Food for Thought 3703463264

What are the moral implications of our attitude to food, and what are the implications of its importance in our culture? This short and accessible book answers questions about the place food should have in our individual lives.

Food for Thought brings together the work of philosophers from Plato to John Stuart Mill, Aristotle to Kant, to help us think about the issues surrounding food. How can we justify the recent explosion of attention given to gourmet food in a world where many are starving? Do we have a duty to be healthy? Are hospitableness and temperance moral virtues? Is the pleasure of good food illusory?

Food for Thought is intended to make those who are involved in working with food think about some of the principles underpinning this field. For those studying philosophy, the book shows how traditional philosophy and some of its classic texts can illuminate an everyday subject.

Educated at Somerville College, Oxford, **Elizabeth Telfer** is Senior Lecturer in Philosophy at the University of Glasgow. She is the co-author (with R. S. Downie) of *Respect for Persons* (1969) and *Caring and Curing* (1980), and (with R. S. Downie and Eileen M. Loudfoot) of *Education and Personal Relationships* (1974), and is the author of *Happiness* (1980).

Food for Thought
Philosophy and food

Elizabeth Telfer

London and New York

First published 1996
by Routledge
11 New Fetter Lane, London EC4P 4EE

Simultaneously published in the USA and Canada
by Routledge
29 West 35th Street, New York, NY 10001

Routledge is an International Thomson Publishing company

© 1996 Elizabeth Telfer
Typeset in Times by Routledge
Printed and bound in Great Britain by
Biddles Ltd, Guildford and King's Lynn

British Library Cataloguing in Publication Data
A catalogue record for this book is available from the British
Library

Library of Congress Cataloguing in Publication Data
Telfer, Elizabeth.
Food for thought: philosophy and food/Elizabeth Telfer.
Includes bibliographical references.
1. Food – Philosophy. 2. Food – Moral and ethical aspects.
I. Title.
B105.F66T45 1996
100–dc20

ISBN 0–415–13381–5 (hbk)
ISBN 0–415–13382–3 (pbk)

To Derek

Contents

Preface

I originally decided to write a book on the philosophy of food because three of my philosophical interests had a bearing on the topic. I was interested in the subject of different grades of pleasure, as it appeared in the writings of several central figures in the history of philosophy, always to the disadvantage of the pleasures of food; I was interested in the nature of the virtues, particularly temperance; and I was interested in the arguments in favour of vegetarianism, which had a personal as well as a professional significance for me at the time when I began the book.

As I worked on it, I found that a discussion of the role in life of food and eating raised many central questions in moral philosophy: the extent of our obligation to the needy, the possibility of duties to oneself, and the place of special obligations in morality. In that respect the scope of the book is wider than the notion of the philosophy of food may suggest. But in other respects it is probably narrower: I have not discussed public policy issues, for example, preferring to concentrate on issues which concern the individual. This is not only because my original interest was in the topic as it affects individuals, but also because a book which tried to cover its social as well as its personal aspects would have become too unwieldy. There is, however, some discussion of the First World's obligations to the Third World.

The approach of the book is traditional, as its origins suggest. Some recent philosophical writing about food adopts a radically different approach: for example, it challenges the assumptions of separateness and 'substance' or thinghood built into the way in which Western philosophers have seen the human person, and it analyses the experience of food (particularly the female experience of food) in ways which, when compared with traditional styles of argument, seem psychoanalytical, or even mystical, rather than philosophical. I have not tried to adopt this approach. Instead I hope to show – to the student of philosophy, to the student who is training for a food profession and to everyone who is interested in food – what traditional Western philosophy can say and has said about this subject.

Acknowledgments

I should like to thank the following for permission to use material from papers which I have already published:

The Editor of the *Journal of Medical Ethics*, for permission to use material from my paper (1990) 'Temperance', *Journal of Medical Ethics*, vol. 16, no. 3.

The Editors and Publisher for permission to use material from my paper (1993) 'The pleasures of eating and drinking', in Dudley Knowles and John Skorupski (eds) *Virtue and Taste*, Oxford: Blackwell.

The Editor of *Philosophical Papers*, for permission to use material from my paper (1995) 'Hospitableness', *Philosophical Papers*, vol. XXIV no. 3.

A large number of colleagues and friends have suggested reading or made points about the topic of food. In particular, Roy Wood of the Scottish Hotel School, University of Strathclyde, sent me his extensive bibliography of food and culture. I am grateful to them all and wish to apologise to those whose suggestions I have been unable to take up. I wish to thank Glasgow University Philosophy Senior Seminar and student philosophy societies at Glasgow, Dundee and Trinity College, Dublin, for helpful discussions of papers I read to them on food topics.

I am particularly grateful to four colleagues. Robin Downie read large parts of the book and made very useful comments. Paul Brownsey and Dudley Knowles helped me with departmental administrative chores to enable me to spend more time on the book. Angus McKay sorted out many computing problems.

My greatest debt is to my husband, Derek Rogers. He has read the whole manuscript and made innumerable improvements to both style and argument, and his help with word processing and editing has been invaluable. Not least, he has been remarkably tolerant of the domestic chaos that I have produced in the course of finishing the book. In love and gratitude I dedicate the book to him.

Introduction

Why are eating and drinking held to be so important? Why do so many newspapers and magazines which are basically not domestic nevertheless carry a weekly recipe or restaurant review? Why are there so many food programmes on radio and television?

At first sight the answer is obvious: eating and drinking are important because they are necessary for survival. But this cannot be the whole answer, any more than the complete answer to the question, 'Why are clothes held to be important?' is, 'To prevent us dying from exposure'. In the case of eating and drinking we can show the inadequacy of the answer by pointing out that they are not in fact necessary for survival. What is necessary is something rather different, namely being fed and watered, and these can happen without our eating and drinking at all: for example, by intravenous drip. If eating and drinking are not necessary to survival but merely one method of feeding and watering ourselves, why do we not save a lot of time and trouble by being intravenously fed and watered during our sleep? The answer is that we think that eating and drinking have a value which goes beyond feeding and watering. This book is in part an attempt to analyse that value.

One element in our belief that eating and drinking have a value which goes beyond feeding and watering is that we view them as possible leisure pursuits. That might seem paradoxical: leisure is surely to be contrasted with what one has to do, so it cannot include eating and drinking, which are necessities of life, any more than it includes sleeping, washing or, of course, work. But my point is that although eating and drinking are necessities (for those without drips and magic capsules, at any rate), they do not need to be treated only as such. To see what this means, let us consider the kind of eating which is often a leisure activity: namely, eating out in a restaurant. If we can understand what makes eating out in a restaurant a leisure activity, we will have some idea of why eating and drinking in general are leisure activities.

The key notion of leisure, as I have already said, is freedom from having to do things. A person is at leisure when he does things which are demanded neither by his work, nor by the necessities of life, nor by his obligations to other people (Telfer 1987: 151–64). In his leisure he chooses what to do, and an important part of that concept is the idea of being oneself and exercising one's individuality. Eating out as a leisure activity, then, is eating out by choice: not as part of work, as when one entertains business guests; nor as daily routine, as for those who eat out all the time; nor in response to a particular necessity, as when the cooker is being repaired; nor as a family duty, as when some visiting relative has to be entertained – but simply because one wants to. Of course one may need a meal, but that is not why one eats *out*.

Why do people want to eat out? The short answer is 'for pleasure': the pleasure of the food, of the surroundings and of the company. And the pleasure of the food includes not only the pleasure of eating it, but also the pleasure of choosing it: the pleasure of exercising one's judgment and taste in selecting what will suit the occasion and combine well together – expressing oneself or being creative, albeit in a simple way. Also characteristic of eating out as a leisure activity is a kind of commitment to the experience, which includes the willingness to spend 'as much time as it takes' – an attitude of leisureliness, if you like.

Can the characteristics of eating out as a leisure activity – the motive of seeking pleasure, the exercise of choice, and leisureliness – play any part in our routine eating? At first sight we may be inclined to think not. We usually eat because we need to; we may have no choice in what we eat if someone else prepares it; and we often eat in a hurry and while thinking of other things. But to some extent we can and do alter these attitudes. We can look for, savour and cherish the pleasures and novelties of our food; we can exercise judgment and taste if we are the cook and not merely the consumer; and we can endeavour to clear the schedule and the mind sufficiently to approach our meals in a leisurely way. To see what I mean, contrast the attitude of someone who comes home tired and strained after work and says to himself, 'As soon as I've had a meal, the evening can begin', with that of someone who says to himself as he sits down to his meal, or even as he begins to prepare it, 'Now the evening is beginning' – or even, significantly, 'Now my evening is beginning'.

For most people, not all meals can be turned into leisure activities in this way. Some meals will have a time limit on them; some will be so interrupted by spouse, children or parents that commitment to the experience is not possible; and some will be so horrible that there is no pleasure to be had. But for many people these difficulties are sometimes avoided, and eating then has some of the flavour of a leisure activity.

However, to claim that eating and drinking can be treated as leisure activities is not to claim that they ought to be treated in this way. It would be possible to claim that they should be treated purely as feeding and watering, and that paying more attention to them than that is short-sighted, decadent or misguided. I shall discuss this claim later in the book.

It might well seem that at the present time the most pressing question about food is not whether eating and drinking can or should be leisure activities – a question which arises only for those who have leisure and plenty of food – but whether a large part of the world's population is to get food at all. In Chapter 1, therefore, I discuss the philosophical problems which attach to the notion of a human right to food, and defend it not only against neo-Malthusians, who argue that giving food aid only encourages disastrous growth in the recipient population, but also against Libertarians, who argue that, because we have a right to do what we wish with our own property, we have no obligation to help those who are starving. But I also argue that there are limits to our obligation to relieve the world's misery, and that among such limits are rights to preserve both happiness and room for self-development through the pursuit of ideals. Eating and drinking as leisure pursuits have a place in the exercise of both these rights.

Chapter 2 tackles the attempt by several philosophers – mostly from the ancient world, but including John Stuart Mill in the nineteenth century – to downgrade physical pleasures such as those of food. I consider their arguments and show that in Greek thought this attitude stems from the notion that bodily things belong to a transient and inferior world, and are therefore of inferior value. I argue that the transience of a thing does not rob it of value, and that the human being is not a disembodied soul trapped in an alien body, but a rational animal to whom pursuits and pleasures with a bodily element are entirely appropriate. But I also claim that the stress which these philosophers place on the pleasure of food, as though that were the only source of its significance apart from its nutritive properties, is misleading, and I explain some of the other kinds of significance which food can have.

In Chapter 3 I discuss in detail one such possible significance for food: I consider whether food can be a work of art, of a kind peculiar to food in being based on taste and smell. This investigation involves a considera-tion of the notion of a work of art in general, and of the difference between art and craft, since cookery is often said to be a craft rather than an art. I dismiss a number of arguments that purport to show that there cannot be an art form based on taste and smell, and conclude that food can be the basis of a simple but minor art form.

Chapter 4 considers the duties concerning food which we owe to others, to ourselves and to animals. I consider the duties of food professionals and the distribution of duties in the household, and argue that the most general duty to others concerning food is the duty to eat healthily oneself, and so be fit to perform one's duties to others. Duties to oneself likewise include a duty to eat healthily, for a parallel reason: good health enables one to perform one's duties to oneself, which consist of the exercise of autonomy and the promotion of self-development in the choice and pursuit of ideals; many ideals involve, in different ways, food and eating. I argue that our duty to animals concerning food is not to eat them. I examine two lines of argument for this conclusion, one based on compassion and the justice of treating animals as we would treat human beings with similar capacities, the other on our essential kinship with animals. I also consider some popular objections to vegetarianism, and conclude that while several of these are more substantial than they seem at first, the reason why people do not adopt vegetarianism is often not intellectual conviction but gluttony.

Chapters 5 and 6 form a pair, examining two moral virtues concerned with food. Chapter 5 discusses hospitableness. Various forms of it are distinguished and tested against Philippa Foot's criteria for a moral virtue (Foot 1978: 1–18). I conclude that while inhospitableness of any kind is an unqualified vice, the positive virtue of hospitableness is what I call an optional virtue, belonging to one particular way of carrying out duties of friendship and benevolence. Chapter 6 discusses temperance, in the sense of the virtue corresponding to the vice of gluttony. I lay down what I call uncontroversial measures of gluttony, distinguish several kinds of temperance, and test them by Foot's criteria. I contend that the only form of temperance that can wholeheartedly be commended as a moral virtue is 'positive temperance', a quality which avoids gluttony on the one hand and insufficient appreciation of the value of the pleasures of food on the other.

My conclusion is a rather guarded one. Having rescued the pleasures of food from their detractors and promoted the claims of food as an art form, I nevertheless want to question whether there is a danger of overestimating the importance of the pleasures of food. Special food is important for significant occasions, and pleasant food is important all the time. But if people expect to eat dinner-party food every day, they run the risk of elbowing out experiences which may ultimately be more satisfying.

1   Feeding the hungry

THE CLAIMS OF THE STARVING

Millions of people, in many parts of the world, are either starving or malnourished. Most of them are in Third World countries, but there are also pockets of severe deprivation in First World countries. For all these people the main question about food is not a philosophical one, but the practical one of how to get enough of it to stay alive and healthy. In what follows I assume that the readers of this book are not in this position, any more than the writer is. For us the pressing question is not 'How are we going to get enough to eat?' but 'What are our moral obligations to the starving and malnourished?' In this chapter I shall discuss not only First World obligations to the Third World, but also the obligations which the well-off have to those in need in their own country.

If nothing could be done to relieve food shortages in the Third World, there would be no moral issue. But probably a great deal can be done – though it is not always easy to work out what. There are two kinds of problem, as the philosopher Nigel Dower explains:

> On the one hand there are disasters of various kinds, like earthquakes, droughts or floods. Emergency assistance is given, people write cheques, and for a moment, there is a strong sense of human solidarity.
>
> On the other hand there is the steady grinding poverty which grips hundreds of millions of people and does not attract media attention. In response to this there are various kinds of programmes, some organized by governments (with or without foreign aid), some organized by charities. These programmes aim to help the very poor escape from their poverty, or to ensure that people do not get into situations of extreme poverty in the first place. These programmes are less glamorous than emergency aid, but their impact is far greater.
>
> (Dower 1991: 273)

So behind the emergencies which capture the public attention there is a long-term need which we must address if we have any obligations at all to the Third World.

Sometimes it is claimed that even the most needy country could feed its population if it did things differently: grew different crops, for example, redistributed its land or settled the internal unrest which stops its farmers from farming. If this claim is true it seems to show that the First World has no obligation to help poorer nations, because their plight is their own fault. However, the claim is not true: many poor countries' problems are the fault of the First World (O'Neill 1986: 111; Dower 1991: 274–5). And even if it were true in a particular case – if, for example, hunger arose from a failure to set aside reserves when supplies were plentiful – it would not follow that the First World has no obligation to help. We think it perfectly appropriate to give help to individuals who genuinely need it, even if their difficulties are of their own making. In the same way we should perhaps help nations whose problems are their own fault – the more so when we consider that the failure is often that of the government, but the suffering falls on the citizens.

According to one school of thought, however, the affluent nations do not have a moral obligation to help the Third World solve its food problems: indeed they have a moral duty not to do so. This view originates with Thomas Malthus, the eighteenth-century writer on population, and is therefore conveniently labelled neo-Malthusian. In the twentieth century it is represented by Garrett Hardin, though not only by him. In his famous paper 'Living on a lifeboat' (Hardin 1985), Hardin compares the rich nations to lifeboats and the poor ones to swimmers wanting to climb aboard. If we in the First World help the poor nations (allow them to climb aboard), we not only enable their populations to increase, we also take away their incentive to improve their own food production and to save food for emergencies. The world population will increase, eventually it will be impossible to support it and the lifeboats will sink. In other words, there will be disaster on a scale much greater than any disaster which now tempts us to let people on to the lifeboat.

This argument is not intended to be an appeal to self-interest. Rather, it bases a moral choice on the lesser of two evils: it is morally better to let relatively small disasters happen now than to bring about enormous ones in the future. This assumes that the issue is to be judged solely on the overall consequences of intervention. Some would challenge that assumption and say that we should relieve now what suffering we can, regardless of the long-term consequences: but this conclusion is as harsh as Hardin's own. Fortunately we do not need to choose between the two conclusions, because Hardin's prediction of the consequences of aid – on which both conclusions are based – does not appear to have any truth behind it. All the evidence shows that when a country's prosperity increases, its birthrate goes down – perhaps because, as infant mortality decreases, people no longer feel they need large families to ensure that some survive (Lappé and Collins 1988: 19–28).

THE HUMAN RIGHT TO FOOD

Having disposed of the argument that we ought not to intervene, we can now consider whether we have an obligation to do so. I suggest we begin not with a philosophical theory, but with what – judging from letters to newspapers and so on – are the typical, pre-philosophical reactions of the 'man in the street'. We cannot end there, because these reactions may turn out to be incoherent, or inconsistent with other moral claims which we are not prepared to give up. But no philosophical account will be plausible unless it makes sense of what people ordinarily feel. And we need to consider not our reaction to the statistics, which most of us find difficult to translate into real terms, but our reaction on those occasions when the realities of the situation are brought home to us. What do we think and feel when we see, on television or in the press, pictures of starving people?

I suggest that many people feel not only compassion (mingled with distress, disgust and a number of other emotions) but also a strong sense that there is something morally wrong. This feeling is different from the one which people have when they see pictures of an earthquake or other natural disaster (unless its effects have clearly been made worse by negligence). It involves the thought that something could have been or still can be done about the situation, and that this action is not a discretionary one but an obligation which some person or persons have failed or are failing to meet.

When photographing disasters, the cameraman often focuses on one suffering individual. This technique has been criticised as sentimental. Perhaps it is, if the person chosen is an unusually pitiful or attractive baby, for example. But if the individual is representative of all, the point being made is not a sentimental one. It is the true claim that the people portrayed are not just a group, an abstract entity which cannot suffer, but individuals, each of whom can and does suffer. And where we think that there is something morally wrong about the situation, portraying individuals in this way can make us realise more clearly that the situation is morally unacceptable, because it is in fact morally unacceptable that any of these individual human beings should be dying of starvation when something could have been done to save them.

The philosophical discourse that deals with these moral ideas is that of human rights. A human right is a basic moral right of paramount importance, belonging to every human being simply in virtue of being a human being, and entailing corresponding moral duties for both governments and individuals. To say that human rights are moral rights is to say that human beings possess them – and ought therefore to be treated in certain ways – independently of whether their government enforces such treatment by legislation. Indeed, part of the concept of a human right is that it provides a standard whereby the level of protection which a government gives to its people may be judged. A human right to subsistence is included among the rights listed in the United Nations' Declaration of Human Rights:

> Article 25. (1) Everyone has the right to a standard of living adequate for the health and well-being of himself and his family, including food, clothing, housing and medical care and necessary social services...
>
> (United Nations 1948: 143–8)

There are, however – and this is the point at which the pre-philosophical beliefs come under philosophical scrutiny – serious difficulties in the idea of a human right to food.

WHOSE DUTY?

I am walking along a deserted country road and see a small child in a pond. It is clearly in difficulties and about to drown. I can save the child by wading in, but I am wearing my new and exceedingly tight leather trousers, which I cannot remove without assistance. If I go into the pond I will ruin them, and there is no help at hand. So I walk on and leave the child to drown.

Everyone will condemn my action, and assume that the child had a right to be rescued. If one can avert a disaster without doing something else wrong, surely one should. And everyone will feel that the loss of my trousers is of no importance in comparison with the loss of the child's life. I suggest that those who are starving have a human right to be rescued just as the child has a right to be rescued, and that they have this right even at the expense of a certain amount of the wealth of the First World, just as the child has it even at the expense of my trousers.

But this analogy, adapted from one suggested by Peter Singer (Singer 1972: 229–43), is unsatisfactory in one respect, one which brings out the single most serious difficulty in the idea of a human right to food: the difficulty of deciding whom the right is against, or in other words, who has the corresponding duty. With the drowning child the duty clearly falls upon me: the rescue ought to be carried out, I can do it and I am the only person who can. Indeed, it is easier to talk of duty than of rights in this case: we are prepared to say that the child has a right to be rescued, but hardly that he has a right against me. But with the rights of starving people the situation is reversed: it seems natural to talk of their rights, but not at all clear on whom the corresponding duties fall.

To clarify this problem a little, no single affluent individual can have a duty to provide for all those in need, since no individual is wealthy or powerful enough. Nor is any single rich man duty bound to provide food for any one poor man simply as a human right, though of course the rich man may have duties to specific people in virtue of specific responsibilities, such as parenthood. Similarly, one affluent nation cannot have a duty to provide for all those in need everywhere, since no nation is wealthy or influential enough; and there is no specific nation which a particular affluent nation has a duty to provide for as a matter of human rights – though a nation might have a special duty to (for example) an ex colony.

The difficulty arises because the human right to food is (in technical language) a positive right, a right to receive goods and services, rather than a negative right, a right not to be harmed or interfered with or restricted. With negative human rights, such as the right to life and liberty, there is no problem about who has the corresponding negative duty: the duty not to interfere with each other person's life or liberty falls on, and can be carried out by, each one of us. And the duty to enforce this non-interference – to maintain law and order – falls on each government, and, since it is relatively inexpensive, can in general be carried out by it.

Can we find a way of deciding on whom the duty falls in the case of positive rights, such as the right to enough food? As we have said, individuals cannot have with regard to positive rights the clearly demarcated kind of duty that they have with negative rights, or the specific kind of duty that they have in a face-to-face emergency like that of the drowning child. But we might claim that individuals have the duty of fostering and supporting a set of organisational structures to meet the needs of the hungry. In that case the hungry could be said to have rights of two sorts: against their government, to have an organised system or structure introduced that will provide for their needs, and against their fellow-citizens, to have their support for such a system. To put it another way, the more affluent citizens can fulfil their duty to the hungry by setting up relief schemes through the agency of their government and pooling their contributions (Downie 1964: 115–42).

This set of rights, duties and mechanisms deals only with the distribution of goods that are under the control of one government. It therefore makes sense only in a country with sufficient resources, taken as a whole, to feed all its people. But that is not an insignificant part of the world: it includes not only poor Third World countries where some individuals have great wealth, but also a great many affluent First World countries, where there are pockets of deprivation. I shall return later to the question of the rights of the hungry in countries that do not have enough resources to feed all their citizens.

Though affluent citizens – in this case – pool their relief contributions to pay for government aid, the government is not their agent in the same sense that a charity would be, because their contributions are not voluntary. But there are many duties that governments may legitimately compel their citizens to perform: because of their importance, because isolated individuals cannot carry them out, or – as in this case – both. If government action is the only or best way in which every needy person in the country can be guaranteed enough food as of right, then the duty of each individual in respect of that right is a duty to campaign for, vote for and support adequate welfare systems. These typically include training schemes and schemes to create employment, as well as handout schemes.

I said above that the first claim of the needy, in a country that can feed its own people, is against their own government and fellow-citizens. This raises two questions: Why, since human rights are rights against everyone, do the needy have a claim against their own government in particular, instead of against the world community? And does their own government have a greater duty to them than it does to foreigners – should a government, in other words, bring its own citizens' standard of living up to a given level before offering help to others? These two questions are most easily dealt with in the form of two similar questions: Is a government entitled to treat its own citizens more favourably than those of other countries, and is it obliged to do so?

Given that it is nation-states that raise and spend revenue and control the distribution of welfare, it is natural to think that the rights of their needy citizens are in the first place against them. From the human rights point of view, we can approve of this arrangement as a more efficient way of looking after people than if help were arranged on a world-wide basis. But people also normally approve of governments which, if they can afford it, offer their citizens a higher standard of living than that demanded by their human right, rather than bringing them up to a human rights standard and then spending the rest of the welfare budget on overseas aid. In other words, people generally approve of governments which show partiality to their own citizens.

The customary justification for giving preference to one's own circle is that it is a natural human characteristic which everyone is entitled to express, and which does not therefore conflict with the essentially impartial nature of morality: we are not saying that Britain may give preference to its own citizens but that every nation may do so. The customary justification of partiality to friends and family in particular is that personal relations are important for a satisfactory human life and for moral development (Blustein 1991: 217–30).

This justification does not straightforwardly apply to a government's favouring its own citizens, but points to two reasons why we can find it morally acceptable. The first is that people often have special feelings towards their fellow-citizens, analogous to those they have those towards their family; and perhaps this relationship, though less intense than friendship and love of family, is an enriching part of human life which governments should foster and give expression to. The second reason is that poor people in a rich country are excluded from normal social life, and may therefore be more wretched and in need of help than materially poorer people in a poor country. So we must conclude that a government has a duty, to some degree at least, to favour its own citizens over those of other countries.

This short account is not meant to suggest that a government that can, in theory, feed all its people will have no philosophical or practical difficulties, even in First World countries, in doing so in practice. Among philosophical problems there is the question of what counts as need: if people can afford enough food only by working at an unjustly low wage, for example, do they need help? And similarly, do people have a right to welfare without making any contribution to it (the 'workfare' issue)? Among practical problems is the fact that a government aiming to ensure that all its people are fed must stay in power and get its policies implemented. If it is to do this without using tyrannical methods that would be as great an evil as the starvation it is trying to prevent, it must have the support of the richer citizens. As we have said, they have a duty to provide this support: but even if they acknowledge this duty in general, they may reject a particular measure if they think it unjust or inefficient. There are also the familiar problems of ensuring that everyone gets enough to eat without creating a 'dependency culture', and of not interfering unduly when attempting to prevent benefits being wasted.

Adequate treatment of these issues would clearly require a chapter each. In this context all I hope to have shown is that the duty of those who are well-off in an affluent society, in respect of the human right of everyone in their own society to have enough to eat, is primarily a political one: the duty to support the institutions by which this can be done. How far this duty extends into our individual lives, and how it is to be evaluated against other demands made on us, are questions to which I shall return.

THE LIBERTARIAN POSITION

There is one group of philosophers for whom the foregoing is an irrelevance, because – they say – there cannot be a human right to subsistence. If there were, governments would be obliged to go beyond their legitimate role of protecting the citizens: they would have to make them contribute, through taxes, to the good of others. This would be to infringe the basic liberties of the citizens and to use them merely as a means of benefiting other people. People who hold this view are known as Libertarians. If what they say is true, the only human rights are negative rights, rights not to be interfered with, as opposed to positive rights to receive goods, and a government's only duty is to respect negative rights and make others do so. (This is a narrow view of the role of government. Usually nowadays even *laissez-faire* regimes, such as the Thatcher government in the 1980s in Britain, see their aims as going beyond protection.)

It might be pointed out that even if the state is not entitled to use taxpayers' money except to protect them, it does not follow that individuals have no obligations to the Third World: what follows is only that any such obligation is not one which the state may compel them to fulfil. However, the existence of individual obligations is not enough to demonstrate that there is a corresponding human right. To be a human right, a right has to be of such importance that governments are obliged to enforce it. In any case, the Libertarian doctrine is not only about the limits of the legitimate scope of governments; it also includes a doctrine about the limited scope of individual obligations which entails that individuals have no obligations to the needy.

The limit to individual obligations ultimately rests on a doctrine about rights to property. According to the Libertarian, our obligations to people in general – those with whom we are in no particular relationship – are to refrain from harming them, but do not include helping them. This is because we have a right to our own time and labour, and to our own property provided it was honestly come by; we are morally entitled to do what we wish with these things (though we may have obligations to specific people arising out of specific relationships). So any donations we make are optional – charity, rather than duty. A compassionate person would make them, but a person who does not is not morally blameworthy.

This combination of a doctrine of limited individual obligations with a doctrine of limited state duties seems to rule out the possibility of a human right to food. We could still say that enough food for all is morally important. But if a right is something which entails that others have duties, there cannot be a right – let alone a human right – to enough food, because neither governments nor individuals have a duty to provide it. At the very least the human right to food cannot be self-evident, as human rights are supposed to be.

One approach to the problem would be to concede the Libertarians' general thesis, but claim that we are not entitled to keep all our property because much of it was not honestly come by. For example, it is sometimes said that the wealth of the ex-colonial powers was acquired by exploiting their colonies, and that they therefore have a moral duty to make reparations. On this view, what is currently given as aid is justified not because it meets an obligation to relieve hunger, but because it compensates for previous harm.

Now it is true that often colonies were developed in ways which benefited the colonial power rather than the colony, and that in the colony industry and trade were restricted. But since we have no way of knowing how any colony would have developed if it had not been colonised, it is impossible to be sure in any given case whether colonisation helped or hindered; so we cannot say that reparations are in fact due (O'Neill 1986: 110). And even if colonisation hindered in general, we have still not shown that it produced food shortages in particular. So this line of argument does not take us very far in showing that we have an obligation to provide food for everyone who needs it.

A second and more promising strategy is to show that the distinction between negative and positive rights is not as sharp as the Libertarian claims. Let us take as an example the negative human right to life: the right not to be killed. This right embodies a recognition of the value of each human life, but that recognition is not worth anything without a positive right to enough food to survive. Similarly, the negative right to liberty is based on the value of exercising one's autonomy. But autonomy requires, as well as the absence of interference, the presence of those basic things without which it cannot be exercised: a social fabric such that a person can have some control over his or her life, and sufficient health to exercise that control. So negative rights and obligations – which the opponents of the human right to food acknowledge – presuppose a foundation for arguing for a positive human right to food.

Anyone who accepts negative rights, therefore, also accepts a basis on which we can argue for the existence of corresponding positive rights. We cannot quite claim that anyone who believes in the human right not to be killed is logically committed to the belief in a right to subsistence; it is theoretically possible to maintain that we are obliged only to avoid making anyone's position worse, not actually to improve it. But a belief in the negative right does imply a belief in the importance of each human life, which makes the step to the positive right a natural one.

A third line of attack is to question the Libertarian's account of people's right to property. Since resources to feed the starving must come from somewhere, a human right to food would entail a limitation on this right, and for the modern Libertarian Robert Nozick this point is enough to show that there can be no rights to subsistence:

> No one has a right to something whose realization requires certain uses of things and activities that other people have rights and entitlements over.

> (Nozick 1974: 238)

Now the basis of such an absolute conception of property rights is weak. First, as everyone agrees, we are entitled to our property only if it was honestly come by. Of course you and I acquired our property honestly, by earning it, inheriting it or being given it; but we cannot be sure that everyone in the preceding chain of owners had such good entitlement. On the contrary, given the moral deficiencies of human beings, we can be reasonably sure that somewhere in the history of our property there was an ill-gotten gain or two. Moreover, it is impossible now to work out how to rectify the situation – and yet we still continue to respect each other's rights to property. What this point shows is that we hold our property not by an absolute right, but as the result of a pragmatic convention.

Second, we must consider how property could have been justly acquired in the first place. Nozick follows the seventeenth-century philosopher John Locke, who starts with the idea that individuals own their bodies and their talents and the products of their talents. They can acquire property by 'mixing their labour with' – appropriating and working on – the earth and its resources, particularly land, which are initially unowned. But each person's appropriation is legitimate only if it leaves others with 'enough and as good'. This theory runs into difficulties when there is no land left: the last person's appropriation cannot leave enough and as good, and is therefore not legitimate, and later comers cannot acquire property at all if all the raw materials are owned. These difficulties can be met – as Nozick agrees – if the landless work for the landowners. This solution implies that the wealth they acquire from waged work will compensate them for their lack of land to work.

This account need not be interpreted as reflecting any real-world events, but there are still many ways in which it fails to show that everybody has been treated fairly. One is that it is only in terms of wealth that the landless are compensated: they cannot choose how to exercise the talents which, according to the above account, they own. Another is that it is not reasonable to compare people's circumstances while there was land available with their fortunes as waged workers – why not instead compare their position under the absolute property system which this account seeks to justify with what it would have been under a modified system? Third, why is it assumed that the land is initially available to all comers on a first-come, first-served basis – why not assume instead that it is owned in common (Locke actually says this, though his story seems to ignore it) and that everyone therefore has the right to a say in its distribution? Without answers to these questions, we are left with an account that does not add up to a justification of an absolute right to property (Kymlicka 1990: 107–18).

I have discussed Nozick's account of the right to property at some length because his theory articulates in philosophical terms a widespread popular idea about property. But many people would also see that this idea can be challenged, and that property rights are not sacrosanct if a sufficiently strong counter-claim emerges. When, in my example, I left the child to drown, no one accepted my excuse that they were my leather trousers and I had a right not to ruin them. This shows that there are situations where life is clearly more important than property.

HUMAN RIGHTS AGAINST THE WORLD COMMUNITY

If a government is unable to feed all its citizens from its own resources, it is meaningless to say that its citizens have a right against the government to be provided with food or the means to get it. We might try arguing instead that the citizens have a right against the world community. Just as, in the First World, children have a right to sustenance against their parents, which becomes a right against the state if the parents are unable to meet their obligations, so (we might argue) all citizens have a right against their own state, which becomes a right against the world community if the individual state cannot make sufficient provision.

It might be objected that 'the world community' is not a moral agent – it has no unity, and so can have no duties. Of course 'the world community', seen as a loose collection of five-and-a-half billion individuals, is not a moral agent, any more than 'the British people' is. But just as the British government can be a moral agent acting on behalf of the British people, so bodies such as the United Nations can be moral agents acting on behalf of the world community – or more precisely, on behalf of its member governments when they have mandated it to carry out some policy. The United Nations has already acted as a moral agent in this way, as when it imposed sanctions on South Africa because of its apartheid policies. In theory, then, it could be mandated to set up systems whereby richer nations help poorer ones, in whatever ways seemed most likely to attain the goal of enough food for each individual, as laid down in Article 25 of the Declaration of Human Rights.

The theoretical situation is thus analogous to that within an affluent country. The poor citizens of an affluent country have rights both against their government, to have a system or structure set up that will ensure that they get enough to eat, and against their fellow-citizens, to have such structures supported. Similarly, the poor citizens of poor countries have rights both against the United Nations, to have a global organisation set up for the relief of hunger, and against other governments, to mandate and support such a system.

However, what we have at present does not add up to a global organisation. Arrangements for giving aid to Third World countries are uncoordinated – each government makes its own – and aid programmes are often criticised. The three main criticisms are that the aid is a hindrance rather than a help, that it has onerous commercial conditions attached, and that it interferes with the receiving government's management of its country.

It is notoriously easy for governments, however disinterested their motivation, to hinder poor countries instead of helping them. For example, they give large amounts of food that destroy the market for the local farmers. Or they provide grants for industrial development, promoting economic growth in the towns, but the profits benefit only a few industrialists, and the poor abandon the land and so less food is grown (O'Neill 1986: 59–62; Dower 1991: 275–6). These problems, which are well documented, and others, do not show that a First World government should never help a Third World country, but only that (as with all giving) it is necessary to ensure that the gift really is a benefit.

Aid is often given in the form of high-interest loans, or on condition that the recipient buys the donor country's goods. These practices are commonly criticised on the grounds that they benefit the donor rather than the recipient, but whether the criticism is justified depends on one's view of the proper role of government. If we think of government as an agent empowered only to serve its citizens' interests, we will conclude that it is not entitled to spend taxpayers' money in ways which do not benefit them. But if, as I have argued, governments are also intermediaries carrying out their subjects' moral duties on their behalf, they may and should help not only their own citizens but also those of other countries, since the duties of people in affluent countries extend beyond their fellow-citizens. This is still consistent with two points I made earlier: that the first duty of a government is to its own people, and that a government is justified in raising its own people's standard of living to a level higher than that demanded by their human rights before giving aid abroad.

The third criticism is that donors of aid impose management tasks on the receiving government – for example by stipulating that it should redistribute the land or institute a programme of population control. In justification it is argued that these measures are beneficial because they improve the long-term prospects of the recipient country, but are donor governments really entitled to attach such conditions? I shall discuss the second example, population control, because it is particularly problematic. It is problematic for two reasons: first, because we might want to claim that there is a human right to procreate, one which is almost as important as the right to enough food; and second, because either donors or recipients may have religious or cultural objections to population control.

We are torn two ways on these issues. On the one hand, it seems wrong for a donor nation to coerce another nation into curtailing its people's rights to procreate, or into doing what it thinks to be wrong, by threatening to let it starve if it does not; and wrong for the receiving government to impose such policies on its people, against their principles and rights, in order to secure aid. On the other hand, it seems wrong to give people aid if the same aid would have produced more benefit elsewhere – that is, by being given to governments that were willing to adopt the necessary policies. This second view does not commit one to the neo-Malthusian doctrine that I mentioned earlier, that aid in itself encourages population growth. All that is being said is that aid is more cost-effective where it is boosted by family planning programmes, and we should choose the more cost-effective option.

If the world community did its job properly, it might be said, there would be enough aid both for communities who are willing to adopt birth control policies and for those who are not. But since the world community operates erratically, and resources are too limited to give all the help that is needed, donors have to make a choice. Is it reasonable to prefer that aid go to those who do adopt measures for population control?

One factor to consider here is that there are more and less invasive ways of controlling the birthrate. The least invasive ways are to educate recipients about reductions in infant mortality, to make it easier for women to work, and to provide advice on natural methods of contraception. Perhaps a recipient government is not being over-coercive if it does these things, or a donor government if it insists only on these things as a condition of aid (O'Neill 1986: 155–8). But a second factor is that coercion is itself an evil, and the more coercive a recipient or donor government's birthrate policies are, the less clear is it that they can be justified even in terms of the balance of happiness over misery. More particularly, the decrease in birthrate attributable to family planning – perhaps as little as 3 per cent – is so small compared with what can be attributed to a general improvement in conditions that it does not justify coercion (Lappé and Collins 1988: 24–5).

THE EXTENT OF INDIVIDUAL OBLIGATIONS

What is the true extent of our obligation, as individuals in an affluent country, towards those in the Third World in need of food? We obviously have a duty to press our government to adopt the best possible aid policies. Beyond that, we might be tempted to think that the question does not arise, because there is nothing that we, acting as individuals, can do.

But this would not be true. In their book *World Hunger: Twelve Myths*, Frances Moore Lappé and Joseph Collins suggest a great many things that the ordinary individual can do (Lappé and Collins 1988: 121–32). (They write as Americans, but the same points apply to Britons and to citizens of other First World countries.) For example, given that the cause of hunger is often political, those who live in a democracy can work through their own institutions to promote policies which improve the position of the hungry. Lappé and Collins claim that abroad this chiefly means removing support from regimes which resist the reforms needed to end hunger.

They also say that we may need to move away from the idea of unfettered property rights. They apply this consideration chiefly to the question of helping those in need at home – presumably they are thinking of our support for taxation to pay for welfare schemes. But a willingness to realise that we may not be morally entitled to everything that is conventionally regarded as our property is equally relevant to helping those abroad. For example, Lappé and Collins say that we can help the hungry in the Third World by the way we shop (where we shop, what we buy and what we refuse to buy) and the way we invest our savings; and that those with relevant skills can help by working in a Third World country. But anyone who believed themselves morally entitled to pay as little, and earn as much, as the free market allows would do none of these things.

Lappé and Collins do not suggest contributing to charities devoted to relieving hunger. This is surprising: the work of Oxfam, for example, or Intermediate Technology – bodies which operate by supporting small-scale local initiatives – seems to be in keeping with their general views. But perhaps they would say that these bodies cannot achieve much by themselves, and that supporting them is a substitute for the political activity that might really make a difference.

Whether we help by giving our time and money to charities or to political bodies, we still need to know how far we are obliged to go. In his well-known paper, 'Famine, affluence and morality', the Australian philosopher Peter Singer starts from the apparently uncontroversial principle that it is wrong not to prevent a bad thing happening if one can do so without sacrificing something of equal moral importance (Singer 1972). On the assumption that it is a very bad thing if large numbers of people starve to death, it follows that we should spend as much time and money on preventing this as we could spend without neglecting any other equally important moral obligation.

This principle, of course, applies not only to helping the starving: it defines our obligations towards relieving other kinds of misery as well, such as the torture of political prisoners. For simplicity, however, I shall treat it as though it concerned only the relief of famine. Good methods of relieving famine – such as cutting off the supply of arms to a civil war – often alleviate other ills as well.

Singer's view is an example of an extreme position which follows from a starting-point that does not seem extreme at all. If we accept it, we seem to be committed to giving away everything which we and our dependants do not need. Even so, this doctrine is not as extreme as the doctrine that the right action is always that which produces the best consequences. That doctrine would oblige us not only to relieve misery, but also to promote happiness. Singer's doctrine, however, says only that we should act to prevent an evil from happening, not that we are obliged to positively promote good, and so is compatible with the view that promoting happiness is a supererogatory action – one which has good consequences but is not obligatory. But there is so much misery in the world that even a doctrine that does not enjoin us to promote happiness still leaves us with plenty of duties to perform.

Nor does Singer's principle entail that I should reduce my circum-stances to penury. For example, I may be able to relieve more misery if I retain my well-paid job and so have plenty of money to give away. But it does entail my asking myself – about each expenditure of time or money

– whether it meets a greater obligation than the obligation to relieve misery. So although there are objections to it, Singer's principle at least points in the right direction, in that it leads us to evaluate conflicting obligations.

Before dealing with the objections to Singer's position, I must make a preliminary point. It is that one cannot refute this kind of position, as people try to do, by showing that its exponents do not live up to it. If they do not, it may cast doubt on their faith in their own doctrine or on their right to recommend it to other people, but it does not show that they are wrong.

There are three main objections to Singer's position. First, there is the objection that such a policy seems to justify any action, provided the results are good enough: even, for example, rigging an election to bring in a party which will institute much-needed land reforms. Second, it may be objected that we have special obligations to our family and friends – for example, an obligation to finance our own children's university education – which limit the general obligation to relieve misery. And finally there is the claim that we have a right to some things of our own which are immune to the claims of others: after all, no one is thought to be obliged to give up a kidney to save a stranger's life.

The first objection applies only if Singer's position is that acts are to be judged only by their consequences, that the relief of suffering is the best possible consequence and that any act which leads to this consequence is therefore the right one. But in his paper, at any rate, Singer does not commit himself to this position. He can therefore reply that running honest elections, or respecting any other rule of justice, is just as morally important as the relief of misery – and add that there are plenty of things we can do to help the starving without breaking important moral rules.

At first it looks as though Singer can handle the second objection in the same way: fulfilling our obligations to our own children is morally as important as helping the starving, so his principle does not entail that we are obliged to spend money or time on the starving at the expense of our children's welfare. But what is the extent of our obligations to our children? The answer to this question depends on how one justifies giving preferential treatment to one's children in the first place. Some people would say that we just feel that our children have a special claim on us. But we must ask ourselves how far we are morally justified in acting on this feeling – after all, not all special favours shown to one's children are necessarily acceptable.

This is a complex and much-debated issue. I shall assume, as most people do, that it is wrong to treat one's children exactly on a par with strangers when distributing one's resources. But there are two possible views on why it is wrong. On one view, special obligations to one's children – and to other groups to which one belongs – represent a justified preference: a partiality which everybody is entitled to practise, and which can therefore be seen as impartial. And we are not only entitled to practise this partiality. In the case of children we have undertaken special obligations to them which require us to give preference to their claims – I shall argue in Chapter 5 that the same can be said about obligations to friends. On the other view, these special obligations are justified by pragmatic considerations: everyone is morally equally important, but in general people fare better if individuals make themselves responsible for the welfare of their own group.

For present purposes, it does not much matter which position we adopt. Those who believe that special obligations represent an impartial and obligatory partiality usually also believe that there is a general obligation to relieve suffering, and that the two obligations limit each other. Those who believe that the end of morality is the equal good of everyone usually also believe that this aim is best served if we forget about it from time to time and do what natural affection prompts us to do; but they would also enjoin us to consider, in our reflective moments, whether we should not spread our benefits more widely. So whichever our theoretical position, we need to weigh up the benefit to our own small circle against the benefit to the wider circle of the hungry.

One cannot give rules for this weighing-up, but one can describe the kind of thinking involved. Let us suppose that I am a wealthy business-woman wondering whether to spend some money on a donation to famine relief or on a sports car for my son. I have an obligation to relieve misery, but I do not have an obligation to give my son a sports car; assertions to the contrary notwithstanding, this is not something he needs for a satisfactory life. Nor is it clear that the world in general is benefited by the practice of giving young men sports cars. So far, then, I should give all the money to famine relief.

However, some of my donation may be wasted if I give it to famine relief, so it may be more rational to give some of it to famine relief and some to my son for some purpose which will not waste it. And if I give my son something which, as well as being owed to him personally, is likely to produce a general benefit, I shall meet both my special obligation to my family and my general obligation to benefit others. Not a sports car, then, but help with his education. This is of general benefit because the existence of well-educated people makes the world a better place.

I find when I examine it in retrospect that this decision is a good one. By dividing my donation and allocating it to these particular ends, I fulfil my duty to relieve suffering; I meet my special obligations to my family;

and I produce a general benefit. I realise that I arrived at this result by exploring ways of maximising the general benefit from the part of the donation that was under my control: the part given to my son. So while it is true that my special obligations have limited the amount I gave to the poor, I have still fulfilled a more general duty to mitigate the effects of that limitation.

Let us now turn to the third objection to Singer's position: that we have a right to some things that are immune to the claims of others. If this objection does not hold, then we have a duty to give to the starving everything we possess, apart from what we need to meet our obligations to family and friends. Most people would not think this, so the objection at least seems to have plausibility.

One possible formulation of it is that we cannot have an obligation to relieve the misery of others if that entails sacrificing our own happiness. Of course, morality sometimes requires individuals to do things which make them unhappy, but such unhappiness is generally thought of as a matter of bad luck, rather than an inherent characteristic of morality. It does not seem reasonable to hold that morality, which on most views is to do with human well-being, could include a general requirement to sacrifice one's happiness.

Even with this limitation, we would still be required to give up any time or money which was not committed to other obligations, if we could spare it without making ourselves unhappy. Many people could spare a considerable amount on these terms, once they had got used to the notion that giving things away does not necessarily lessen one's happiness, and indeed often increases it.

But we can claim more than just the right not to sacrifice our happiness: we can claim the right to a personal space in which to pursue the worthwhile life. Someone might claim, in other words, that whereas he would be perfectly happy giving all his spare money to Oxfam and all his spare time to addressing envelopes for them, he was not obliged to do so because such a life was not the most worthwhile one he could lead. It was not the most worthwhile because it gave no scope for self-development, no scope for cultivating his talents and no scope for doing what is valuable in itself rather than merely useful.

Now most people would concede that this person was not developing his talents, and that this was a bad thing. In fact we can put it more strongly than that. In general we disapprove of people who do not make the most of themselves or who have no self-respect or independence – even if we think they are happy enough – and moreover we are ashamed if we detect these traits in ourselves. This general disapproval suggests that we have not merely a right, but a duty to cultivate our talents, develop ourselves and do what is valuable in itself – in other words, to pursue the worthwhile life. (I shall discuss this question further in Chapter 4.) And that requires us to have a personal space in which to do it.

INDIVIDUAL OBLIGATIONS AND THE WORTHWHILE LIFE

This discussion of Singer's position has yielded a number of considerations which limit our obligation to relieve suffering. First, we are not bound to relieve suffering if doing so would flout some more important moral principle; second, we are entitled to give precedence to our obligations to family and friends; third, we are entitled to provide for our own happiness; and fourth, we are allowed to pursue our own self-development, cultivate our talents and engage in the worthwhile life.

These limits on what we should spend to relieve suffering are important for the theme of this book, because they allow us to be interested in food ourselves. To put it more explicitly, the considerations that limit our obligation to relieve suffering also justify us – despite the strength of the competing moral claims on our resources – in spending more time and money on our own food than will simply keep us healthy. If we are entitled to safeguard our own happiness, we are entitled to have sufficiently pleasant food to keep us happy; and if we are entitled to pursue the worthwhile life, then we are entitled to pay more attention to our food than mere happiness requires. We can pursue gourmet cooking, for example, as a way of cultivating a talent or practising an art, and we can produce and enjoy good food as part of the wider personal ideals of style and elegance, hospitality and friendship. I shall take up these ideas in later chapters.

The claims of the starving seem now to have been whittled down by competing considerations to the point where they have no force at all. What remains of the human right to enough food? Rather more than might appear: for we still have to justify everything we do against the claims of the starving and what we might instead do for them. I have argued that, apart from relieving hunger, we are morally entitled only to relieve other suffering, to fulfil any moral obligations that have a higher priority, to preserve our own happiness and to pursue a worthwhile life. But these entitlements still leave us with ample time and resources for meeting the needs of the starving, if only the will were there.

2 The pleasures of food

THE EVERYDAY PURSUIT OF THE PLEASURES OF FOOD

In the last chapter I concluded that, despite the demands made on us by the hungry and others in distress, we have some space in which we are not obliged to think only of obligations to others. This space is marked out by two rights. These are the right to safeguard one's own happiness and the right to lead a worthwhile life: to do what is worthwhile and to be a worthwhile person. In this chapter I shall begin to consider the role which food and eating might play in this space. This theme – the role of food in the worthwhile life – will feature in later chapters too.

Let us note to start with that most twentieth-century Westerners devote more time, money and attention to food than is needed to stay alive, or even to stay healthy and active. We do this because we think that as a result our food will give us a great deal of pleasure. This claim does not entail the implausible view that the more money one spends on food the more delicious it is. On the contrary, since the spending includes time and attention as well as money, the claim is perfectly compatible with the widely held belief that with ingenuity one can eat both cheaply and deliciously.

But we may sometimes wonder whether we should pay less attention to food and more to other things. No doubt this question naturally occurs to those who cook regularly, but many people must have thought about it at one time or another. If, for example, we come across people who pay less attention to food than we do ourselves, we wonder whether in this respect their way of life is not only different from ours, but also better.

This is not just an everyday, ordinary person's question. There is also a long-standing tradition in Western philosophy, dating back at least to Plato, which throws doubt on eating and drinking as sources of pleasure. This tradition has two strands. One – the quantitative strand – maintains that the amount of pleasure produced by eating and drinking is not as great as it seems. The other strand is qualitative: it maintains that the kind of pleasure to be got from eating and drinking is less worthwhile than the kind that is to be got from other pursuits. If we want to justify the trouble we take over food in terms of the pleasure it gives, we need to refute both these doctrines.

PRELIMINARY QUESTIONS

We must first dispose of four problems which seem to be inherent in any philosophical discussion of the quantity or quality of pleasure. The first problem is whether we can speak intelligibly about comparing quantities of pleasure. All we can say is that people do; they talk about getting more pleasure from one thing than from another, or enjoying something more or less than they used to. This is all that is needed to give the idea meaning.

The second and more serious problem is this: can we separate the pleasures of eating and drinking from other pleasures? In typical situations where we enjoy eating it is very difficult to work out how much of our enjoyment derives from the food itself and how much from the company or setting. The difficulty arises because the pleasures of the food and of the company are not merely simultaneous experiences: they also enhance and modify each other. I enjoy the wine more because I am sharing it with Robert Redford, and so on.

This seems to me to be a real difficulty. The best we can do is to try to mentally isolate the pleasures of food. We might for example focus on those occasions when we eat alone with pleasure, or compare the pleasures of eating in company with the pleasures of doing other things in company. I think this kind of thinking enables us to form a rough idea of the pleasures of food as such. But I shall suggest later that the pleasures of food also have an important role as enhancers of other kinds of pleasure.

A third difficulty with the question of how much pleasure we get from food is that it seems to be an empirical question, one to be answered by psychological research in the field, rather than a philosophical one, to be answered by thinking in the study. Moreover, it may have as many answers as there are people: can there be an answer to questions about how much pleasure people in general, as distinct from particular people, get from food? Philosophers often wrongly ignore difficulties of this kind. But on this occasion I would argue that there is no problem, on the ground that the facts about the nature of the pleasures of food are too well-known to need testing in the field and sufficiently general to transcend any differences between individuals.

The fourth and final difficulty is the most important: is it possible to be mistaken about the extent of one's own pleasure, as the quantitative doctrine seems to assume? I think that it is. I do not mean that someone else can know more about my pleasure than I do myself when I assess it honestly. But it is possible to enjoy doing something without realising it at first, and become aware of the enjoyment later, for example when someone interrupts the activity and one finds that one is reluctant to stop. Mistakes about pleasure are possible, then, and so it is not nonsensical to claim that we all overestimate the amount of pleasure given by food.

THE QUANTITATIVE STRAND

The quantitative strand in the arguments against the pleasures of food is the claim that the amount of pleasure we get from food is not as large as we are apt to think. If this claim is valid, having pleasant food does not make such a significant contribution to our happiness as we might suppose.

One argument for this claim concerns after-effects. Those who indulge in the pleasures of the table, it is said, suffer from indigestion and hangovers in the short term and ugliness and ill-health in the long term, and these miseries outweigh the pleasures. This is not a cogent argument, because with care these ill-effects can normally be avoided. So for people who enjoy their food and drink, the risk of misery is worth taking: in terms of quantity of pleasure the bet on food is a good one. Perhaps people have a duty to not even risk their health or looks for the pleasures of food, but this objection is not relevant to the question of what brings the greatest quantity of pleasure.

A second argument of the quantitative kind is that the pleasures of food are vulnerable: people can lose their teeth or digestion, or the money which enables them to eat and drink pleasurably. But this is not an argument against the pleasures of food in particular. All pleasures are vulnerable, but a person who loses his capacity for one particular kind of pleasure can get pleasure from other things. So the prudent policy is to lead a mixed life, with many different sources of pleasure. If we do this, the vulnerability of the pleasures of food – or of any other kind of pleasure – does not matter.

One might nonetheless object that there is bound to be pain at losing any source of pleasure, even if other pleasures compensate for the loss; so the vulnerability of the pleasures of food makes it wiser to leave them out of the combination. This argument presumes that the pleasures of food and drink are more vulnerable than other kinds of pleasure, but this is not obviously the case. It is true that people can lose their teeth and digestion – but they can also lose their sight, hearing and mental capacities. Which happens more often: that people become blind, deaf and senile, but still able to enjoy their food; or that they lose the ability to enjoy their food, but can still think, see and hear and talk to their friends? This is an empirical question, and the answer is not obvious. We must conclude that the pleasures of food are at least as likely to survive as the contemplative pleasures which tend to be regarded as absolutely safe.

A third quantitative argument, used by Plato, portrays the pleasures of eating and drinking as a kind of addiction. Plato claims that seeking pleasure from food is self-defeating: a person who does this is never satisfied, and gets less pleasure each time (Plato 1979: 491e–4e).

Now there are four different ways in which eaters might be said to be never satisfied, and in order to meet this attack we must distinguish them. First, there are normal eaters, who are temporarily satisfied but soon want to eat again. Then there are gluttons, who always want to be eating but who enjoy their food. Third, there are epicures, who have to have something out of the ordinary before they can enjoy what they eat. And finally there are addicts, who for present purposes are people who feel compelled to eat or drink more and more, but do not enjoy it. (It is their lack of enjoyment which makes us call their behaviour addictive rather than simply gluttonous.)

Now we can describe all these people, including normal eaters, as 'never finally satisfied'. But the phrase is ambiguous: it can mean either that they never really enjoy their food or that they never feel they have had enough. It is true that for those who feel the first kind of dissatisfaction – namely the addicts and the epicures, for whom the pleasures of eating or drinking constantly diminish – food is a poor source of pleasure. The gluttons and the normal eaters, however, can be described as 'never satisfied' only in the second sense. The gluttons want more all the time, the normal eaters satisfy their appetites temporarily but later want to eat again. But unlike the epicure and the addict, both gluttons and normal eaters (most of us, I assume) continue to get pleasure from their food.

Unless we are addicts or epicures, then, the fact that our desire for food is never finally satisfied does not mean that food produces less pleasure than we think. On the contrary, the constantly renewed desire for food is a positive advantage from the point of view of quantity of pleasure, and the fact that we can temporarily have enough a disadvantage – one which, it is said, the Romans tried to remove by making themselves vomit during banquets so that they would have room to eat more. There may be a tendency for people who appreciate the pleasures of eating and drinking to become epicures or addicts. But this danger besets other kinds of pleasure too: people can become compulsive readers or jaded devotees of culture. The pleasures of eating and drinking, at any rate, are sufficient to make the risks of addiction or epicuredom, though worth looking out for, risks worth taking.

The fourth and most important argument of the quantitative kind is that spending money, time or effort on food is not a cost-effective way of getting pleasure. The same expenditure could have procured far more pleasure of other kinds, it is alleged, particularly as the pleasures of food are comparatively short-lived. For example, I can spend three-quarters of an hour on preparing a meal which gives me only fifteen minutes' pleasure, or I can open a tin and be able to spend the three-quarters of an hour on something itself enjoyable, such as watching a good television programme. Or again, I can spend ten pounds on a meal in a restaurant which gives me pleasure for an hour, on a theatre ticket which gives me pleasure for two-and-a-half hours, or on a paperback novel which gives me pleasure for six hours. In all these cases, isn't food the poorest bargain from the point of view of pleasure?

Supporters of the pleasures of food might say that, as far as time and effort are concerned, food is a good bargain. This is because there is actually no cost: they get pleasure from preparing food as well as from eating it. But this reply is unconvincing, because it ignores what the philosopher Jeremy Bentham in the early nineteenth century called the fecundity of some of the competing pleasures: that is, their capacity to produce more pleasure at a later time (Bentham 1962: 64–7). If I learn a piece of music, see a play or read a novel, these experiences live in my mind and produce other pleasures – I remember the works and contemplate them again; I see the world in a different way because of them. None of this seems to be possible with the pleasures of eating and drinking. As we shall see in the next chapter, food can be an art form, but it does not have these possibilities: I can recall flavours and textures, but I cannot contemplate them later or gain a new idea of the world in terms of them. In the light of these considerations, the claims of aesthetic and intellectual activities to be more cost-effective sources of pleasure than eating and drinking seem strong.

Despite these points, which are after all fairly obvious, a great many people spend a lot of time, trouble and money on getting food they enjoy. Doubtless some of them have never stopped to think about the best ways of maximising their pleasure. But there are also those who think carefully about how to enjoy themselves and who give a prominent role in their enjoyment to eating and drinking, and if the argument that the pleasures of food are not cost-effective is true then they are behaving irrationally. We can try to make sense of their apparent irrationality in two ways.

The first way is to suggest that on many occasions the pleasures of eating and drinking are cost-effective, despite appearances, because their intensity compensates for their brevity and lack of fecundity. But given the intensity of some aesthetic pleasures which are also very fecund, this claim is not plausible.

The second way is to suggest that the pleasures of eating may be a kind of pleasure for which there is no substitute. I have written hitherto as though pleasure were a commodity which could be desired in the abstract, independently of its source, so that anyone who is seeking pleasure must rationally prefer what gives more of it to what gives less. We often do talk in this way: 'I decided I got more pleasure out of golf than out of the clarinet,' someone might say, 'and since I haven't got time for both, I've given up the clarinet'. On the other hand, pleasure is closely bound up with its source. This means that some kinds of pleasure, for some people, cannot be adequately replaced by other kinds of pleasure; and for many people it seems that the pleasures of food are of this kind.

THE QUALITATIVE STRAND

Some philosophers hold that it is unworthy to show a particular liking for the pleasures of food. In their view eating may be a good source of pleasure, but it is not a source of good pleasure. This is the second strand of doctrines in the Western philosophical tradition attacking the pleasures of food – the qualitative as opposed to the quantitative strand. In effect it maintains that while food is necessary, our enjoyment of it is not one of the elements that makes up a worthwhile life.

One argument of this kind is that since eating is only a means to an end, namely survival, the pleasure it brings must have a lower status than the pleasure of those activities which are ends in themselves. This argument fails because its premise is false. Certainly eating is a necessary means to survival. But, as we have seen, the eating which goes on in any affluent society consists of a great deal more, in both quantity and quality, than survival requires, so it is clearly more than just a means to survival.

But probably the best-known example of the qualitative strand of arguments is to be found in nineteenth-century English philosophy: in John Stuart Mill's doctrine of higher and lower pleasures, which he lays out in his essay 'Utilitarianism' (Mill 1962a: 257–62). Mill divides pleasures into two kinds: mental pleasures, which employ the intellect or the imagination, and physical pleasures, which do not.

We must first make clear what Mill means when he says that some pleasures are higher or, as he sometimes says, better than others. He does not mean that some pleasant activities and experiences give us more pleasure than others; that would be a matter of quantity rather than quality. Nor does he mean that there are some pleasures which we have a moral duty to prefer to others. Mill's claim is that the better pleasures are more worthwhile or more worth having; they are what an enlightened person prefers. This conception of worthwhileness is distinct from both quantity of pleasure and duty: a person can value one pleasant experience more than another while acknowledging that the second gives him more pleasure, and he can pursue for its own sake the pleasure which he values more, without thinking in terms of duty at all. So it is a claim about the quality of pleasure.

Mill says that we know which kind of pleasures are the higher pleasures by observing which kind competent judges prefer – competent judges being those who are 'equally acquainted with, and equally capable of appreciating and enjoying, both [kinds of pleasure]' (Mill 1962a: 259). We find, he says, that they always prefer the mental pleasures. So far so good; but Mill goes on to declare that anyone who does not prefer the mental pleasures has lost his capacity to judge! This prejudging of the issue by ruling out any judge who gives the wrong answer suggests that Mill does not regard the verdict of the judges as the ultimate criterion of quality, but instead has some other basis in mind. It is therefore simpler to leave out the notion of competent judges altogether and look directly at the considerations which lead Mill to downgrade the physical pleasures.

Mill's true criterion, though he does not make it explicit in 'Utilitarianism', is that the physical pleasures of eating and drinking, and of sex, are inferior because they are shared with the animals; they do not employ our 'higher faculties' – what he calls 'the distinctive endowment of a human being' in the essay 'On liberty' (Mill 1962b: 187). Mill claims that no one would choose a life without the pleasures which only human beings can have: 'few human beings would consent to be changed into any of the lower animals, for a promise of the fullest allowances of a beast's pleasures' (Mill 1962a: 259). He attributes this refusal to a sense of dignity, which – he says – is so strong in most people that they cannot be happy if they do or suffer anything which conflicts with it.

However, Mill's doctrine is mistaken. First, it is not clear what is meant by his claim that the pleasures of eating and drinking are physical rather than mental. All pleasures are mental, in the sense that they all depend on consciousness. It is true that the pleasures of eating and drinking have a physical source, in that they depend on input from the senses; but so do many so-called higher pleasures, such as looking at art or nature, or listening to music. Perhaps the pleasures of food are more crudely physical than these, in that they involve physical interaction between the body and what is enjoyed. But though this makes them less rarefied, it does not rob them of their mental element.

Second, his argument that pleasures of food are inferior because they do not employ man's distinctive endowment is very unsatisfactory. In the normal human being the pleasures of food do in fact employ man's distinctive endowment; they are quite different from those of a pig at a trough. The human uses his mind to appreciate combinations of flavours and textures, the suitability of the food for the season, the craftsmanship of the well-prepared dish, and so on. And even if it were true that the pleasures that humans get from food were similar to the pleasures that animals get from food, why should we assume that those pleasures are therefore inferior? Why should we assume, in other words, that the activities and pleasures which are distinctive of our species are more valuable than activities and pleasures which are not? If we believed in a beneficent God whose purposes we respected, and who designed us for a task which other creatures could not fulfil, we would have reason for such an assumption. But if we have no such belief, why should we not cast off the burden of rationality and aim at a more pig-like condition?

Mill claims, however, that our sense of dignity would not let us choose a pig's life. Now it is probably true that most people would choose a discontented human life rather than a perfectly contented pig's life. But a typical human life has so-called physical pleasures as part of it, so such a choice would not necessarily show that we thought the higher pleasures more valuable – it might only show that there were some higher pleasures which we were not prepared to give up. (There might also be some lower pleasures which we were not prepared to give up.) The real question which Mill's claim raises is this: if one had the choice between, on the one hand, a normal human life, with both 'higher' and 'lower' pleasures in it, and, on the other, a life consisting purely of 'higher' pleasures, would our sense of dignity demand that we choose the latter? Mill's doctrine suggests that it would.

To see what this choice would mean, imagine that an eccentric millionaire arranges his life so that he never needs to eat (he is fed intravenously) or to move (because movement gives physical pleasure). He sees beautiful things through television cameras, but never climbs mountains or walks round galleries. He listens to music, but does not play an instrument or sing, because there are physical elements in the pleasure of doing these things. Nor does he go to concerts, because the pleasure of concerts partly depends on the physical proximity of other listeners, and this factor would introduce a non-intellectual element. He converses with friends, but does not touch them. He reads, but turns the pages by remote control because handling paper is a tactile, and therefore 'lower', pleasure. Suppose a person spent his life like this, and suppose we waived questions about whether he had a duty to be getting out and about in the world. Would it be the perfect life, or not a human life at all?

One possible view is that it would be both non-human and the perfect life. Aristotle, for example, claims at one point that the ideal life, one spent in contemplation, is too godlike for human beings but nevertheless a goal towards which we should aspire (Aristotle 1980: X, 7) – in other words, the less like human beings we can be, the better. This view is in fact rather uncharacteristic of Aristotle, who usually says that the proper goal for a human being is a life which is characteristically human. Another possible view is that such a life is theoretically achievable and contains all that is necessary for a valuable human life; on this view there is nothing essentially animal about human life. This is the view that Plato held, as we shall see.

But my guess is that 'few human beings', to use Mill's phrase, would regard such a life as even as good as human, let alone better than human. I do not simply mean that we would consider it intolerable. I mean that we would despise rather than admire someone who chose to live in that way, judging them to be unhealthy and perverted, and would say that the animal pleasures – or rather the complex interplay of the physical and the intellectual which constitutes the so-called 'lower' pleasures in a human being – were a valuable part of human life. Humans are a rational sort of animal, and 'animal' pleasures as we experience them are as appropriate to human beings as intellectual pleasures are. In other words, our 'sense of dignity' itself would lead us to reject the millionaire's way of life on the grounds that it was not worthy of a human being.

FALSE PLEASURES

In Greek philosophy, the best-known example of the qualitative strand of arguments is Plato's doctrine of false pleasures. He expounds this in the *Republic*, and it is a particularly striking attempt to show that the pleasures of food are not worth having. Plato argues that many so-called pleasures, among them the pleasures of eating and drinking, are not genuine pleasures at all, but only reliefs from pain which we mistake for pleasure. The only genuine pleasures are those which do not depend, as the pleasures of eating do, on a previous desire (Plato 1955b: 583b–7b).

This argument can be interpreted in two ways. On one interpretation, the pain in question is the physical pangs of hunger, and Plato is saying that we mistake relief from these pangs for a positive pleasure. There are several things wrong with this claim. First, it fails to distinguish the physical state (cessation of the pangs of hunger) from the mental reaction to it. Second, it fails to recognise that this mental reaction can take more than one form: I can be pleased that my pangs of hunger have subsided, but I can also be indifferent (if something else claims my attention), or even distressed (if their disappearance is the symptom of some disorder). Third, it assumes that the pangs of hunger can be removed only by eating. But this is not the case: they can also be removed in other ways, for example by drugs. Fourth, it assumes that the pleasures of eating and drinking are dependent on a person having felt hungry previously. But this is not true either. There are unexpected but keen pleasures of eating, such as that of eating wild raspberries on a country walk, which do not depend on previous hunger and are very like the pleasure of smell which Plato mentions as an example of a genuine pleasure (Plato 1955b: 584b).

The second interpretation of Plato's argument postulates that when he writes of the pain which is relieved, he is referring to the psychological longing for food, rather than the physical pangs of hunger. On this interpretation, his thesis is that many of our so-called pleasures are only relief from the pain of desire, a desire which ceases as soon as we obtain the thing we want; genuine pleasure occurs only when the source of it was not previously desired. But this is not a satisfactory argument either: desire is sometimes pleasant rather than painful, and getting what one previously wanted does not always bring even apparent pleasure. So on neither of these interpretations can we argue that the pleasures of eating and drinking are not genuine pleasures.

PLATO'S ACCOUNT OF HUMAN BEINGS

Plato's underlying thought in the doctrine of false pleasures seems to be that because eating fulfils a bodily need, the pleasures of eating are illusory, in that they depend on the body being in a disordered state, in need of repair. It is as though ordinary living is a disorder which produces a false idea of the pleasures of eating, in much the same way as illness sometimes distorts our appetite and sense of taste. This view of sensory experience as unreliable is central to Plato's account of human beings. According to Plato, the self or true person is a non-corporeal, rational, immortal being. This being is essentially independent of the body, but temporarily housed in it – trapped, one might even say – and awaiting release by death. For Plato, ultimate reality is the non-material realm of the Forms or essences of things, which are universal and eternal; the everyday world is only half-real, not truly existing, 'becoming': in other words it is constantly changing and decaying, and possesses no characteristics except in a qualified way. Since knowledge properly so called is about the Forms, and not about the material world, it follows that it is through his or her rational self that the philosopher – the most developed type of human being – possesses knowledge, rather than through the world of sense-perception to which our bodies and of course their food belong. The following passage gives a vivid idea of Plato's picture of human life:

> The lovers of learning find that philosophy takes their souls in hand – for their souls are simply bound and glued in the body, and compelled to survey reality through the body as through a prison wall, instead of freely by themselves, and they are wallowing, moreover, in utter ignorance; and philosophy sees that the body-prison in its cunning works through desire, contriving to make the prisoner aid and abet his own imprisonment as much as possible. The lovers of learning, then, as I say, find that philosophy, taking over their souls in this condition, gently soothes and tries to free them, pointing out that the evidence of the eyes and of the ears and of the other organs of sense is thoroughly misleading, and urging them to withdraw from the use of the senses except when such use is inevitable. It encourages the soul to gather itself up into itself, all alone, and to put trust in nothing but itself – to trust only such realities as it may discern in their essential nature by its own essential nature; whatever it sees by the use of something else, things appearing variously in various other things, it should count in no way real. Such things are objects of sense and visible, while what the soul sees by itself is an object of thought and invisible.
>
> (Plato 1955a: 82d–3b)

This passage is from the *Phaedo*, the dialogue which depicts Socrates, just before he dies, arguing for the immortality of the soul and urging his friends to 'practise death' by separating themselves from bodily concerns as far as they can (Plato 1955a: 80e). When they ask him how he wishes to be buried, he replies, 'You will need to catch me first!' (Plato 1955a: 115c).

As the contemporary American philosopher and classicist Martha Nussbaum shows in her book *The Fragility of Goodness* (Nussbaum 1986), Plato's doctrines in the *Phaedo* and *Republic* are related to a preoccupation of Greek thought: the sharp awareness of the vulner-ability, physical and moral, of human beings, combined with the hope of a way of becoming, through reason, self-sufficient, invulnerable and immune to luck, and of securing goods which are truly worth having, because they are somehow safe and permanent in an unpredictable world. Against such a background, things belonging to the body tend naturally to be downgraded, though, as I tried to show earlier, the things of the mind are not immune to luck either.

This kind of thinking is familiar to us in ordinary life today through its echoes in Christianity. Although Christianity is about the Word made flesh, Christians are told to renounce the world, the flesh and the devil, and the injunction to renounce the flesh is still honoured rather literally in such traditions as giving up sweets for Lent and by groups which practise self-mortification.

In philosophy, as Nussbaum says (Nussbaum 1986: 4–5), a Platonic tradition about personhood and value persists to this day (alongside other traditions) because of the great influence of the eighteenth-century philosopher Immanuel Kant. According to Kant, the only thing which has dignity – a value which is beyond price – is morality, and humanity so far as it is capable of morality (Kant 1948: 102). For Kant, morality is the exercise of the good will which (if it is possible at all, and Kant admits that we cannot know that it is) is a free, non physical activity which cannot be constrained by physical causes. Here is Kant's secular equivalent of the treasure laid up in heaven which 'neither moth nor rust doth corrupt' (Matthew 6, 20); like the treasure in the Gospel, Kant's treasure beyond price is available to all and cannot be taken away.

In this climate of thought it is easy to see why the pleasures of food might be regarded unfavourably. Is there any way of bringing food into the sphere of reason? We can study food chemistry and thereby make food the subject of a science with universal laws, but this approach leaves out our subjective experience of food. Or we can decide that cookery is an art and food an art form (I shall discuss these topics in the next chapter) and thereby hope to give food a value which transcends the pleasures of the present moment. But a more promising approach than either of these is to reject the whole Platonic outlook, insist again that we are rational animals, and value the goods that suit that state on the grounds that they are fit for human beings.

There are two reasons for rejecting the Platonic account of human beings. One is that it relies on a sharp distinction between human beings and the rest of the universe; but this distinction has been made less and less plausible by advances in our knowledge of other animals. We may be more rational than the apes, but the difference now looks like a difference of degree – albeit a large one – rather than a difference of kind. The other reason is that in the twentieth century philosophers have come to believe that the doctrine that soul and body are separable is not tenable. There are intractable problems about how immaterial souls could be individuated. But also philosophers have argued that words referring to mental qualities and activities are about what we, as embodied people, do in the public world, not about private activities in our heads. (Incidentally, this movement in philosophy is a return to Christian orthodoxy, not a rejection of the whole Christian hope: Christianity speaks of the resurrection of the body, not of the immortality of the soul.)

As Nussbaum points out, Aristotle generally depicts us as rational animals and maintains that we should live as such. Except in his uncharacteristic commendation of the life of trying to live like gods, he argues that the good which we should seek is the good for human beings, not some abstract 'Form of the Good'; the fact that this lasts for ever, he crisply says, does not make it any better than other good things (Aristotle 1980: I, 6). For Aristotle, knowledge of how to live is derived from practical wisdom, which depends in the end on particular judgments and a kind of perception, rather than on reason and universal principles.

In his account of the virtue of *sophrosune* or temperance, Aristotle shows that physical pleasures, including the pleasures of food, have a place in human good. The exercise of moral virtues is part of the good for man, he says, and to exercise the virtue of temperance one must have a capacity for physical pleasure. This does not simply mean that if we did not enjoy food we would have no need of temperance. Aristotle thinks that the virtuous person takes pleasure in the practice of virtuous activity; in other words, people are not temperate unless they enjoy their temperate eating as well as practising it. Nor would we be more temperate, and therefore better people, if we did not mind what we ate: a person who did not like some foods more than others would be defective, not human, he says (Aristotle 1980: III, 11) – and here he clearly thinks that not to be human is not a good thing.

The Greek awareness of the fragility of mortal things, as Nussbaum makes clear (Nussbaum 1986: 2–3), was accompanied by a realisation that they have a special beauty of their own. This idea finds expression in Greek thought in the many myths of gods falling in love with mortals. But are mortal things in fact especially precious? It is true that for us they have their own kind of poignancy. The pleasure we take in flowers, for example, is coloured by the fact that they bloom one day and wither the next. Likewise the moral beauty of an action can depend on mortality – there would, for example, be no such thing as giving one's life for someone else, if people lived for ever. But to say that mortal things have their own kind of poignancy is not to say that they are necessarily better or more beautiful or more valuable. Aristotle's observation that lasting for ever does not make the Form of the Good better than other things is a tool that cuts both ways: if eternal things are not better for being eternal, it follows that mortal things are not better for being mortal.

It also follows, of course, that mortal things are no worse: that they are no less valuable than changeless things, and that they are characteristic aspects of human life which it would be unbalanced to ignore. Given these points, we might argue that a full human life, while trying to cater for the longing for permanence, ought also to do justice to the things which belong to mortality. And this brings us back to the pleasures of food: if we adopt an Aristotelian rather than a Platonic attitude to ourselves, we shall find no reason to despise the pleasures of food.

THE MEANINGS OF FOOD

So far the discussion of the role of food and eating in the pleasant and the worthwhile life has been entirely in terms of the pleasures of food. This is because the philosophers I have been discussing, both those who wished to downgrade the role of food in life and Aristotle who wished to re-establish it, saw the issue in these terms. Plato thought that the reason why people were tempted to pay a great deal of attention to food was simply that it gave pleasure, and so he saw his task as that of undermining this particular pleasure. Mill was writing in the Utilitarian tradition, in which pleasure was the sole measure of value. If he wanted to maintain that physical activities were less valuable than intellectual ones, despite the great amount of pleasure they clearly produced, he had to express this point by saying that physical pleasures were lower pleasures. (Most commentators would claim that in saying this he is actually forsaking the pure Utilitarian position.) Aristotle rehabilitates the physical pleasures in the context of his account of the virtue of temperance, which he defines as the virtue concerned with the desire for the pleasures of food, drink and sex.

However, this emphasis on pleasure is misleading: people also value food and eating for many other reasons. I am not simply making the obvious points that we value food because it keeps us alive, and that we can use meals as opportunities to do something else, as with the business lunch. The eighteenth-century philosopher and theologian, Joseph Butler, said, 'Everything is what it is and not another thing' (Butler 1970: 14). Despite Butler, I shall claim that food and eating, at any rate, are what they are and often many other things as well, and that we often value them because they are these other things, not because the food tastes good. To explain what I mean, I shall list some of the ways in which food and eating can also be other things. I do not claim that the list is exhaustive, or that the divisions between the categories are clear-cut.

First, a meal can be a religious observance. One example of this is the traditional Jewish Passover meal, in which elements of the food symbolise elements in the story of the Jews' escape out of Egypt. The Christian sacrament of Holy Communion is religious eating too, but it is a less clear-cut example, because the eating and drinking there are merely token eating and drinking rather than a meal in their own right.

Second, eating in a particular way can be a statement, and indeed a celebration, of one's allegiance to a particular religion, race, nation or region. A Hindu who refrains from eating beef may do this both for religious reasons and to express solidarity with his heritage. Similarly a Scot who eats haggis on Burns Night may not actually like haggis (or Burns), but feel that in doing so he is showing who he is and how much it matters to him to be Scottish.

Third, a person's choice of food can be an assertion of his values and principles. The vegetarian is obviously asserting a principle in his choices: less obviously, the non-vegetarian is doing so too. People can also be making a broadly political statement in eating or not eating particular foods – as when they buy the products of a fair-trade co-operative or refuse to buy those of an exploitative company – or when they buy local produce rather than imported produce.

Fourth, a meal can celebrate a present or past event. A graduation, a coming of age, a marriage, a new job, for example, are in themselves somewhat abstract happenings which we can be pleased about but cannot enjoy, but by associating them with a meal we turn the abstract event into one that we can enjoy. It is true that food does not have to be involved – we can celebrate with a hill walk or a concert, for example – and the reasons why we so often choose food are doubtless very complex. But obvious considerations are that everyone enjoys eating and that everyone can do it, so a celebratory meal does not exclude anyone.

Fifth, eating together regularly is a way in which a group, be it a family, a regiment or a college, fosters unity and feelings of loyalty. Eating together has a powerful bonding effect, over and above the fact that the occasion brings people together in the literal sense. Going to such meals can also be a statement of one's values and principles, as noted above: in going regularly I am in effect saying that my family, college or regiment is important and that its solidarity should be upheld.

Sixth, preparing meals for others or eating meals with them are often acts of friendship and love. A friend, parent or lover wants to give things to the loved one, and a common gift is food, whether made by the giver or not. Similarly, friends and lovers want to do things together, and one of the things they often do is to eat together. Because food is essential to life itself, giving it and sharing it seem to have a special significance. It is as though we are saying that we want to give the most important thing of all to the person we love, or to share the most important activity with them.

Seventh, a meal can be an exercise in civilisation, style, elegance or luxury. For example, those who kept up formal British ways of eating in the jungle, in the days of the British Empire, thought of themselves as maintaining the standards of civilisation amid barbarity. Whether this kind of behaviour is in fact civilised is of course another matter – it might rather be thought of as a piece of chauvinism and arrogance. Not everything that food stands for is a good thing.

Finally, a meal, or a dish in it, can be seen as a work of art. I shall discuss this idea in detail in the next chapter.

In some cases the significance of food and eating depends on the eaters' intentions, and in others not. Empire-builders can be arrogant in their eating without intending to be so, and a person can be stylish in her eating without thinking of being stylish. On the other hand, rituals and celebrations require that the participants see them as such – though there might be borderline cases, as when a student eats a luxurious meal he cannot afford on the evening after the examinations, and when asked about it says, 'I suppose I was unconsciously celebrating'. I assume that making a moral statement has to be deliberate. But a vaguer act, such as 'showing where you stand', might not be: whether or not they think of themselves as doing so, non-vegetarians show where they stand on eating meat by eating it.

I have made much of the idea that eating is often not just that but also other things as well. But this feature is not peculiar to food and eating. Perhaps – despite Joseph Butler – everything can be what it is and other things as well, and there is nothing especially significant about the meanings of food. Just before writing this, for example, I watched a father, accompanied by his young son, putting money into a savings account in the son's name. That action could also be an act of love, an assertion of a belief in the importance of saving and self-reliance, part of a celebration of the boy's birthday or of some achievement of his, and so on. Is there any point in claiming that food can be what it is and also other things if the same claim can be made about everything?

I think it may be true that everything can be many things in this way. But there are three reasons why it is worth emphasising the point with regard to food. First, my aim is to strengthen the case against a school of thought which devalues the importance of food in our lives. That school of thought expresses its position in terms of an attack on the pleasures of food. In addition to defending the pleasures of food against this attack, I wish to show that there are many other points of view from which food might be regarded as important. Second, we may be particularly tempted to ignore the other dimensions of food because utility and pleasure are such obvious features of it. And third, I think that the fundamental nature of food makes it a particularly important vehicle of other kinds of significance.

Not everyone has a savings account. But everyone eats, so nobody who has any choice about their eating can avoid making some of the other choices and statements which food expresses. If I never eat with anyone else, that says something about me. If I never eat a proper meal but only snacks, that says something too. If my food is exactly what I would eat if I lived in California, although I live in Glasgow, that says something too. This universality is not unique to food: the same kind of thing could be said about dress, for example. But there are very few other spheres of activity which are so general that virtually everyone can be appraised in terms of their handling of them.

In stressing the aspects of food that are not related to pleasure, I am not suggesting that there is something suspect about enjoying one's food, and thereby falling into the same error as my opponents. On the contrary, the pleasures of food are an important part of life, even when we consider them in isolation, and enjoyment plays an essential part in some of the other meanings of food which I have been listing. A celebratory meal, for example, expresses the joy of the participants about what is being celebrated, but it will not do that satisfactorily unless it is an enjoyable meal. Again, if I give a meal to someone I love, its chief significance for both of us is the feelings I express, but I shall try to make it a particularly enjoyable meal precisely in order to express these feelings.

Finally, we must remember that the pleasures of food are not usually found in isolation, although I have discussed them in isolation in this chapter. They are usually combined with other kinds of pleasure, 'higher' or 'lower', to the advantage of both pleasures. We can drink wine while we read or listen to music, picnic while admiring a landscape, dine while we converse, and find that each pleasure enhances the other. This capacity for combining with other pleasures seems to me to be one of the most important aspects of the pleasures of food.

3　Food as art

FOOD AS ART

In the previous chapter I suggested that food and drink might sometimes constitute an art form, and in this chapter I shall consider that question more directly. Philosophers who have dealt with this topic tend to say that whereas food and drink can of course produce aesthetic reactions, it cannot be an art form or produce works of art. I shall therefore begin by examining the concept of aesthetic reactions, in general and as applied to food. I shall then consider the concepts of a work of art and an art form, and show how these concepts might be applied in the sphere of food. I shall go on to discuss the reasons which philosophers have produced for rejecting the idea of an art of food, and consider how they may be countered. Finally, I shall briefly discuss the social significance of regarding food as an art and some reasons for concluding that it is a minor rather than a major art.

AESTHETIC REACTIONS

What makes us call a reaction an aesthetic one? We naturally associate the word 'aesthetic' with the arts, but we can also speak of an aesthetic reaction to natural things such as a beautiful landscape, or to man-made, non-art objects such as pieces of machinery. J. O. Urmson, in a well-known article (Urmson 1962), takes for granted that an aesthetic reaction is not a neutral reaction, but a species of pleasure. He suggests that we can best distinguish an aesthetic reaction from other kinds of reaction on the basis of the grounds for it. For example, if we react favourably to a play because it will earn a lot of money for us, because it teaches a fine moral lesson or because it is a successful venture for a playwright we know, our reaction is not aesthetic. Our reaction is aesthetic, in many simple cases, if it is based solely on how the object appears to the senses.

This appreciation of a thing for its own sake is sometimes characterised as disinterested. The use of this word is misleading: my favourable reaction to the play because I am pleased by my friend's success might be called disinterested, but it is still not an aesthetic reaction. The point is better made by calling the reaction non-instrumental: I appreciate the thing's look or sound for its own sake, not for any benefit it brings to me or others.

Now, as Urmson himself says, it is not at all clear how this account can be made to apply to aesthetic reactions in more complex cases. For example, our appreciation of a novel does not seem to be sensual; still less our appreciation of the beauty of a logical proof (which Urmson allows as an example of an aesthetic reaction). However, his account fits those reactions which are likely to be most nearly like our reactions to food. If I admire some factory chimneys because they make a marvellous pattern, my admiration is aesthetic, whereas if I admire them because they show the factory to be powerful, it is not. Similarly, if I like the way cottage cheese contrasts in flavour and texture with rye bread, my reaction is aesthetic, whereas if I am pleased with the combination because it is low-calorie and high-fibre, it is not.

Are all cases of non-instrumental liking of a sensual phenomenon aesthetic reactions? We think of aesthetic reactions as needing also to have intensity: vaguely saying 'that's nice' without really taking something in does not seem to deserve the name. But the requirement of intensity does not imply that aesthetic reactions always involve actively paying attention to or concentrating on something. This is true of deliberate aesthetic activity, but some of the most powerful aesthetic reactions involve being impressed by some unexpected or short-lived phenomenon – perhaps something too quick to pay attention to, such as a flash of forked lightning. Nor need there be any analysis of what is seen or heard. Often analysis does take place, as when I see the fields in a landscape as forming a pattern. But suppose I lie on my back in the grass on a cloudless summer's day and gaze up into the sky, as if wallowing in the blueness. There is nothing to analyse, but surely this is an aesthetic reaction.

So far I have not challenged Urmson's assumption that an aesthetic reaction is a pleasant reaction to something. But it will not do as it stands. An aesthetic reaction need not be a favourable one, and even where it is, pleasure may not be the right characterisation of it. For example, we might speak of being interested or intrigued by a pattern of clouds, excited or exhilarated by lightning, moved by a panorama, awed by a natural wonder such as Niagara Falls, and so on. In none of these cases is 'pleasure' the right description of our feeling, though sometimes 'joy' would be appropriate.

Often we claim a kind of objectivity for our aesthetic reactions. We can say of both man-made and natural objects not only 'I am excited, moved, awed by this', but also 'This is sublime, beautiful, elegant, intriguing', as if attributing a quality to the object. Sometimes the second way of speaking may be only another way of expressing our own reactions, as when I say 'This is nice' as I get into a hot bath. But at other times we think of the object of our aesthetic attention as in some way warranting or meriting a particular reaction, because it has qualities which other people also would appreciate or come to appreciate in it. In other words, there is often a sense of objective judgment in our reaction. This sense of objectivity need not entail a belief that some things are beautiful, graceful or awe-inspiring in themselves, regardless of how human beings see them; perhaps aesthetic qualities are capacities which some things have to arouse reactions of a certain kind in us. But it does mean that the realm of the aesthetic is not all 'just a matter of what you like'. We think that there can be judgments in this sphere which claim to be in some sense valid or well-founded, and that it makes sense to argue about them, even if the arguments often cannot be resolved.

It might be objected that the word 'judgment' is scarcely appropriate to describe a sudden reaction to a flash of lightning. However, I did not claim that there is an element of judgment in every single aesthetic reaction. My wallowing in the blueness of the sky need not be accompanied by the thought that everyone ought to feel as I do about it, any more than my reaction to the lightning need be. But in each case judgment is possible: one might say to oneself immediately afterwards, 'How beautiful!' and think of the sight as deserving one's feeling of joy.

Aesthetic judgments can sometimes be made in the absence of the non-neutral reaction which normally accompanies them. In some states of mind I can look at a landscape which would normally delight me and feel quite indifferent to it, but still see it as beautiful – meaning, perhaps, that it is the kind of thing which ought to delight people, and would normally delight me too.

The account which I have given of aesthetic reaction will not suit all cases. But I hope I have succeeded in suggesting a range of sense-experiences which fall under the description of 'aesthetic reactions', and which may be characterised as non-neutral, non-instrumental, having a certain intensity and often accompanied by judgments for which the judgers claim a kind of objectivity.

How does all this apply to food and drink? Urmson is rather grudging on the matter: 'It is at least reasonable to allow an aesthetic satisfaction to the connoisseur of wines and to the gourmet' (Urmson 1962: 14). There are, however, some more specific points that one would want to make.

First, it is generally agreed that there can be aesthetic reactions to tastes and smells. (There can also, of course, be visual aesthetic experiences connected with foodstuffs, as when one admires a rosy apple, but these raise no questions peculiar to food and drink.)

Second, as with the other examples of aesthetic reaction, we can distinguish liking the taste and smell of food from approving of it instrumentally on the grounds that it is nourishing, fashionable or produced by politically respectable regimes. Likewise we can distinguish the person who 'enjoys his food' but does not notice what he eats, from the person whose awareness is more vivid – the latter reaction being the only one which is characteristically aesthetic.

And third, as with the other senses, the non-neutral, vivid and non-instrumental reaction to tastes and smells can be combined with a judgment for which the judger claims objectivity. I can not only like a food myself but also believe that the taste is a fine one which people ought to like, even if some of them at present do not. For example, I may not only prefer fresh grapefruit without sugar myself, but also think this preference is justified and hope to convince others of this. It is also possible for the judgment to become detached from the non-neutral reaction, as with other kinds of aesthetic reaction: I can say 'These sandwiches are good' when I am aware that they deserve to be enjoyed but I am so tired that I am quite indifferent to them myself.

WORKS OF ART

As I said earlier, many philosophers argue that although food and drink can give rise to aesthetic reactions, they cannot constitute works of art. In order to examine this claim, we first need to consider what is meant by saying that something is a work of art.

Not all objects that can give rise to aesthetic reactions are works of art. A work of art is by definition a man-made thing, even if the human involvement need consist of no more than putting a natural object in a gallery and giving it a title. This much is clear, but beyond this point there are considerable complexities. One problem is that the phrase 'work of art' can be used in either a classifying or an evaluative way. To use it in a classifying way is to say something about how the object is regarded, whereas to use it in an evaluative way is to say something about the extent to which it merits the label 'work of art'.

Urmson's definition of a work of art takes the phrase in a classifying sense: for him a work of art is 'an artefact primarily intended for aesthetic consideration' (Urmson 1962: 22). Since we know from our discussion in the previous section what is meant by 'aesthetic consideration', we can now expand this definition: if something is a work of art, then its maker or exhibitor intended it to be looked at or listened to with intensity, for its own sake. So if I go into a gallery of modern art, see a pile of metal pipes in a corner and wonder whether it is a work of art or some materials left behind by the central heating engineers, I am employing Urmson's sense of the phrase, wondering whether the pile is intended to be looked at with intensity. However, Urmson's use of the word 'primarily' allows for the possibility that a work of art might be made for use as well as ornament. So a chair can count as a work of art if the maker intends it primarily to be looked at in the way one would look at a picture, even if he also intends it to be sat upon.

The classifying sense of the term 'work of art', in the way Urmson uses it, takes the maker's or exhibitor's intentions as the criterion for deciding whether something is a work of art or not. There are, however, objects such as ethnological objects, or religious buildings, which were not intended by their makers as works of art but which are now treated as such. So we have a second classifying sense of 'work of art': a thing is a work of art for a society if it is treated by that society as primarily an object of aesthetic consideration.

To grasp the evaluative use of the phrase 'work of art', consider again the pile of metal pipes in the gallery. Suppose I look at it more closely, and find a notice on it saying 'Modern Times' or 'Metallic Three' (or even 'Metal Pipes'); I may now say 'That's not a work of art, that's just a pile of junk'. I know perfectly well that the pile is a work of art in the first sense: that is, I know that the artist and the gallery owner intend us to gaze at it with intensity and that the public will probably oblige. But I am claiming that this object is not worth gazing at in this way, that it does not merit or repay aesthetic consideration.

People who use the phrase 'work of art' in this evaluative way are from one point of view commending the things that they call works of art, but it does not follow that they consider all works of art to be good ones. Thus the person who refuses to call a collection of pipes a work of art might also say of a not very good conventional sculpture, 'That is a work of art, even if it's not very good', meaning that it deserves to be appraised aesthetically, even though it may then be found wanting.

The distinction between the classifying and the evaluative senses of the phrase 'work of art' is relevant to food. I shall claim that some dishes clearly constitute works of art in the classifying sense. But I shall also discuss arguments purporting to show that food does not merit aesthetic attention: in other words, that dishes cannot constitute works of art in the evaluative sense.

So far I have written as though there is no problem about what philosophers call the 'ontological status' of a work of art: what kind of a thing it is, what kind of existence it has. But in fact there are many problems. Perhaps buildings, pictures and sculpture are unproblematic (though even here there are difficulties about the case of many identical etchings taken from one plate). But a piece of music is not a tangible object at all: for example, the Moonlight Sonata is not the piece of paper on which Beethoven wrote it, since there is still such a thing as the Moonlight Sonata even if that paper is destroyed. On the other hand, we do not want to identify the sonata with its performances, not only because it is one thing and they are many, but also because it would exist as a work of art even if it had never been performed. The same sort of thing can be said of plays. We therefore have to see this kind of work of art, a piece of music or a play, as an abstract thing, a kind of blueprint for performance. This point has relevance to food, as we shall see.

We can now begin to consider whether it makes sense to say that food and drink can sometimes be works of art. First I must clarify the question. It is obvious that foodstuffs can be made into visual objects which are works of art. The great pastrycook Carême – who was famous for the immensely elaborate models (known as *pièces montées*) which he made out of sugar and other foodstuffs – once said of confectionery that it was the principal branch of architecture (Quinet 1981: 164–5). It could be argued that these objects are not food, since they were not intended to be eaten, but food properly so called is likewise often arranged or decorated in creative and attractive ways which constitute a visual work of art. However, the taste of food and drink as well as the look of it can give rise to aesthetic reactions, and I therefore wish to ask whether food and drink can sometimes constitute works of art of a kind peculiar to themselves, appealing mostly to the senses of taste and smell.

Our definition of a work of art, in the classifying sense, was: 'a thing intended or used wholly or largely for aesthetic consideration'. This is not true of run-of-the-mill food. But many meals are intended by their cooks to be considered largely in this way – to be savoured, appraised, thought about, discussed – and many eaters consider them in this way. Such meals also serve the functions of relieving hunger and providing nourishment, but they are of a kind which shows that this is not the main point of them. A meal that claims to be a work of art is too complex and long-drawn-out to be understandable in terms simply of feeding, and a cook who has cooked a work of art is not satisfied if the eaters do not notice what they eat. Such a cook aims to produce a particular kind of pleasure, one which depends upon a discerning appreciation of the flavours and how they combine and succeed one another.

To illustrate the approach of the cook who prepares a work of art, I quote from *The Good Food Guide Dinner Party Book* (Fawcett and Strang 1971). This is a book of recipes collected from some of the restaurants recommended in *The Good Food Guide* and assembled by its authors into suggested dinner-party menus.

Guests who are particularly interested in food and cooking would enjoy this meal with a savoury beginning and fruity finale... The deep-fried croquettes are made of haddock and creamed potato. Serve them with sauce tartare... since its cold sharpness is a foil for the smoked haddock's savoury richness...

(p. 62)

With all this richness [roast duck with port and orange sauce or pickled pineapple or prune and Beaujolais sauce] try a green salad and the rather bland puree of potatoes and chestnuts...

(p. 101)

...the result is a homely rather than an elegant sweet, with the sharpness of the cherries contrasting with the mildness of the filling.

(p. 101)

The Jaegermeister pâté is a forceful one, with venison and liver as the basic ingredients, seasoned with mushrooms, herbs and brandy. The salad served with it is an agreeable contrast of crisp apples, celery and walnuts in mayonnaise.

(p. 106)

Instead of muffling the scampi in a coating of crumbs, this recipe prescribes a delicate cream sauce, flavoured with mushrooms and brandy, which complements their flavour perfectly.

(p. 106)

These passages and many others like them illustrate the authors' desire to design dishes, courses and whole meals which present patterns of harmonious or contrasting flavours and textures. This is the approach of the cook who is designing a work of art.

ART, CRAFT, CREATION, INTERPRETATION

I have so far discussed cookery as an art, but perhaps cookery is really a craft. So we need to know what the difference is between art and craft.

Some commentators draw the distinction on the basis of the purpose to which the artefact is to be put: if it is intended for contemplation it is a work of art, if for use it is a work of craftsmanship. This distinction employs the notion of a work of art in what I called the classifying sense. But this way of drawing the distinction is not satisfactory. As we have already seen, something which is incidentally useful may be primarily intended for contemplation, and things not intended for contemplation by their makers are sometimes treated as works of art by others.

There is another possible distinction between art and craft: art is original creation, whereas craft is carrying out an instruction, following a convention or employing a technique (Whittick 1984: 47–52). This distinction is between kinds of work, rather than between the products of the work. We can apply the distinction without difficulty to some cases: for example the architect who designs the church is an artist, whereas the masons and woodcarvers who carry out his instructions are craftsmen. But other cases are less clear-cut. Painting and composing are normally thought of as original creation, but painters and composers often follow a convention: they create in accordance with a set of rules which defines a genre, such as sonata form or the conventional iconography of paintings of the Virgin Mary. If following a convention is the mark of a craftsman, then painters and composers are often craftsmen in that respect. But unlike the exact instructions of the mason, such conventions leave room for choice, so the painter's or composer's use of them is both craft and a part of the creative process. The same feature of craft in art is seen if we consider technique. Technique is a mark of craft, but the creative artist requires technique: we can distinguish creativity from skill in brushwork in painting, and creativity from mastery of orchestration in composition. Again, the painter's use of technique is both craftsmanship and part of the creative process.

The conclusion that emerges from this discussion is that the distinction between art and craft is basically not between people but between different aspects of their work, which may be blended in different proportions; if the work contains a good deal of creativity it will be thought of as art, if it contains a modest amount it will be thought of as craft, but there is no sharp distinction. The extreme case of the mason leaves no room for creativity, and so the mason is a craftsman who is not an artist at all; we might class him as a technician. But many so-called crafts, such as pottery and furniture making, leave plenty of room for creativity alongside the following of a convention and the employment of technical skill.

This blend of creation and craft applies also to interpretation. People tend to speak of composing and writing plays as creative, playing music and acting as interpretative. This way of speaking suggests that interpretation is not creative and is therefore not art. But the interpreter is in a position rather like that of a composer or writer writing in a genre with a strict convention. The music or drama that is being interpreted does not provide an exact plan of what is to be done, so interpretative artists have to make choices, have to be creative, and within an interpretative art we can distinguish between creativity and technique. In a sense, then, each performance is a work of art. If we do not use the phrase 'work of art' in this context, it is perhaps because we have a sense that a work of art must be something durable – an idea to which I shall return.

So is cookery an art or a craft? It is true that it is often thought of as a craft. One reason for this is that its products are useful. But as we have seen, the usefulness of a thing does not prevent its being a work of art, so this criterion does not prevent cookery from being an art. And if the distinction between craft and art is based on the degree of creativeness, some cookery can still qualify as an art. As we saw from *The Good Food Guide Dinner Party Book*, recipes are sometimes treated as works of art, of a kind analogous to musical compositions. The cook who creates such a recipe is a creative artist. A cook can also create recipes by producing variations on someone else's recipe or on a traditional one, like a jazz composer arranging a standard tune or a classical composer arranging a folk song; cooks who do this are also creative artists.

Those who actually produce the dishes may or may not be artists. If a chef who creates such a dish gives exact orders for its preparation to his team of assistants, the assistants are technicians rather than artists, and the relationship between chef and technicians is like that between the architect and the masons. But most cooks are like neither architects nor masons. A cook following a recipe (a recipe that is a work of art, that is, like those in *The Good Food Guide Dinner Party Book*) is normally a performing artist rather than a technician, because recipes are usually vague ('season to taste', 'add a pinch of ginger if desired' and so on) and need interpretation. So a particular cook's version of a recipe is an interpretative work of art, like a particular musician's performance of a piece of music. The same applies if the creator of a recipe cooks his own dish; he is an interpreter as well as a creator, like a composer playing his own compositions. (Both will of course need technique as well as interpretative artistry, such as the ability to make a white sauce without lumps, and pastry which remains in one piece.) It might seem as though the cook following recipes rather than creating them has room for artistry only when the recipes are vague. But even the cook who follows precise recipes has to make choices about the combination and sequence of dishes in a meal, and so to that degree is an artist.

DISHES AS WORKS OF ART

If cookery is an art form, what exactly is the work of art?

I said that both an original recipe and an actual dish (a particular performance of a recipe, as it were) are works of art if they are regarded aesthetically. However, sometimes there are problems about this scheme. Suppose a chef working for Marks and Spencer creates a superb pie, which is then turned out by the thousand. Are all the pies works of art, or is the abstract recipe the only work of art? The nearest analogy in the standard fine arts is probably with engraving and other forms of print-making, where the essence of the process is that it enables an artist to produce many copies of one work. Since we can call each engraving a work of art, we can call each Marks and Spencer pie a work of art, at least in the classifying sense.

There is another problem of quite a different kind about the status of dishes as works of art. Because people have to eat them to appreciate them, and because each person necessarily eats a different part of the dish, it might seem that in the sphere of food no one can appreciate a complete work of art, and no two people can appreciate the same one. I am not referring to the common thought that all viewers and listeners approach works of art from their own points of view and with their own preconceptions, and so in a sense each sees a different work of art. The present problem, if there is one, belongs particularly to food, and is more like a situation where each viewer of a picture sees only one section of it.

In fact, however, a dish of food is normally more homogeneous than this, or should be. All those who partake of it are presented with roughly the same thing. What they smell and taste is tangible stuff. But it is not a structure with parts, even if the dish is a structure with parts, like a pie, because one cannot smell or taste a structure. Admittedly there may be problems where a dish is not homogeneous enough: one diner's experience of the strength and blend of flavours may not match another's. These accidents are comparable to having a seat in a concert hall from which some of the instruments in the orchestra are inaudible: the recipe is not at fault, but the performance is.

Another apparent difficulty about treating dishes of food as works of art is this: how can there be works of art which are destroyed by the very activity, eating, which is necessary for contemplating them? This difficulty too depends on the mistaken idea that what is appreciated is a structure. As before, the answer to the difficulty is that even where a dish is a structure such as a pie, the aspect of it which is relevant to aesthetic appraisal is not the structure, which is destroyed as soon as the dish is started, but the combination of flavours, which runs right through the eating like letters through a stick of rock (Prall 1958: 185).

OUGHT FOOD TO BE AN ART FORM?

So far I have not mentioned art forms. An art form is a type of work of art, a class to which works of art in a similar medium belong. For example, sculpture is an art form, the class to which the particular works of art that are sculptures belong. So if dishes of food are works of art, then food is an art form. The term 'art form' has the same two senses, classifying and evaluative, as the term 'work of art'.

It would be implausible to maintain that food and drink never constitute works of art in the classifying sense. People sometimes treat them as works of art, and I have argued that we can compare the creator of a recipe to a composer, and the cook who follows one to a performer. But some philosophers are willing to go further than this and claim that food deserves to be treated as art. D. W. Prall seems to be claiming this when he says.

> Like all sense presentations, smells and tastes can be pleasant to perception, can be dwelt on in contemplation, have specific and interesting character, recognizable and remembrable and objective. They offer an object, that is, for sustained discriminatory attention.
>
> (Prall 1958: 187)

But others have claimed that there cannot be such a thing as an art of food as there is of painting or poetry. Since food is in point of fact sometimes treated as an art, these philosophers should be construed as saying that food and drink do not repay being treated as works of art: in other words, that food is not an art form in the evaluative sense. Of course, we can agree that much food is not. But I shall argue that the reasons for dismissing the whole sphere of food from being an art form in the evaluative sense are unconvincing, although I shall eventually conclude that, as an art form, food and drink are a minor one.

The first argument against food and drink as works of art in the evaluative sense concerns the usefulness of food and drink: it might be claimed that nothing useful deserves to count as a work of art, because, as Oscar Wilde said, 'All art is quite useless' (Wilde 1948: 17). This argument must be fallacious: of the traditional fine arts (architecture, sculpture, painting, music, poetry) one, namely architecture, is concerned with useful objects. The proper point to make about the uselessness of art, as we saw at the beginning of the chapter, is not that works of art must be useless things, but that to appraise an object aesthetically is to consider it in abstraction from its usefulness. Whether a thing, useful or not, can be a work of art in the evaluative sense depends on whether it is worth appraising in this way.

However, perhaps those who say that food should not be treated as art because it is useful are really claiming that abstracting from usefulness is particularly difficult in the case of eating and drinking. One might reply that, on the contrary, it is all too easy to forget about usefulness (that is, nutritional value) when eating, and what is difficult to forget is the urge to simply munch away without thought. Either way, what these points would show is that it is difficult to treat food as an art form, not that it never merits being treated in that way.

Or perhaps the argument about usefulness is really that it is inappropriate to look at food aesthetically because this is treating a means as an end, and assuming food to be positively good when it is merely necessary. This argument is similar to those used to demote the physical pleasures. But it will not do. It is food as nourishment which is necessary, but the aesthetic value of food depends not on its nourishing properties but on its taste and smell. What we are valuing aesthetically is in effect a different thing from food as nourishment.

A second reason for refusing to count food as a work of art in the evaluative sense relates to the physicality of the way we appreciate food. Whereas we can see and hear at a distance, we taste something only if it actually touches the relevant parts of the body. Isn't this (it might be said) too crude to be art? We might retort that sight and hearing also require a physical link between thing perceived and the organ of perception: light waves in the one case, sound waves in the other. It remains true that the contact between the thing tasted and the taste-organ is direct in the case of food – but why should this matter? The question, surely, is not whether the way we taste things is crude but whether tastes themselves are crude. One might as well say that music played on a violin is cruder than music played on an organ because the violin is a simpler instrument.

As we shall see shortly, some philosophers do wish to argue that tastes are too crude to sustain art. But the argument from physicality, if I may so call it, might have a different origin: it might stem from a sense that the body taints what it is associated with, and that the freer we are of it the better we are. Sight and hearing, on this view, are nobler senses because they are less physical, and to cultivate the more physical kinds of perception is to concentrate on unworthy objects. And of course taste is not only physical in the sense of being dependent on physical contact: normally (except at a wine-tasting or similar) we taste things in the course of making them part of our bodies. So anyone who thinks that we should as far as possible ignore the body might well feel that to dwell on any element of the processes by which it is renewed is in some way disgusting.

As we saw in Chapter 2, this hostility to the body is found in Plato, Aristotle in his Platonic moods and some strands of Christianity. I argued there that their arguments should be rejected. If we do this, we will reject along with them the argument that the physical nature of the sense of taste makes it unworthy.

But can combinations of flavours be sufficiently complex to constitute works of art in the evaluative sense of the phrase? Many writers think they cannot. One set of claims is that the eye and the ear are capable of finer discriminations than the senses of taste and smell; that the eye and the ear have more powers of recuperation; and that it is difficult to remember tastes (Gurney 1880: 10–11). These claims depict the limitations as being in us. Another set of claims is that tastes cannot be arranged in regular patterns, and that they do not possess form. These claims depict the limitations as being in tastes themselves.

The distinction between limitations in us and limitations in tastes is itself problematic. How can we be sure that a limitation is in the tastes and not in our perception of them? Does this distinction even make sense? But even if we accept the distinction for the sake of argument, what these considerations show is not that food cannot constitute works of art, but a much weaker thesis: that works of art based on food must be relatively simple. It is instructive that Monroe Beardsley, when discussing the possibility of works of art in food, asks why there are no 'taste symphonies and smell sonatas' (Beardsley 1958: 99). Symphonies and sonatas are exceedingly complex works of art. He should have asked whether there can be taste-and-smell preludes, and the answer is by no means so obvious.

Let us start with the arguments that depict the limitations as being in us, and more particularly the claim that in taste and smell we cannot discriminate finely. It is true that our sense of smell, at any rate, is less highly developed than that of many animals. But we can still recognise a huge range of different smells and tastes. Moreover, these capacities can be developed and trained: we have only to think of the skills of the wine-taster or tea-taster. If our culture laid more stress on the importance of discrimination in food, more people would cultivate a palate, in the same way as musicians train the musical ear. The results might still be cruder than the discernments which can be made in sights and sounds, but this would not show that an art of food could not be worthy of the name. An artist can deliberately restrict his range of colours and shapes, or sounds and timbres, and still produce beautiful works.

The effect of the alleged limitations in our powers of recuperation is this: after tasting something very bitter or strongly spiced, say, we cannot for a while taste anything more subtly flavoured. But there are analogous problems in other arts. After loud ringing chords, the ear finds difficulty in focusing on small sounds; if we look too hard at a bright red shape in a picture, we find that shape, in green, floating about in front of our eyes as we look at the rest of the picture, and so on. In all these cases, artist and audience each have to make allowances. We learn not to stare at one part of a picture, and the conductor or pianist learns to leave a pause after loud chords. Similarly the chef serves a sorbet, or the diner eats a piece of bread, 'to cleanse the palate' after the goulash. There seems to be no difference in principle here, even though there may be a greater limit to the abruptness of possible contrasts in the realm of food. What these limitations suggest, if they exist, is not that there cannot be an art of food, but that such an art must be simple.

As far as our allegedly limited memory is concerned, it is not clear what the limitation is supposed to mean. If the claim is that memory is needed to enable us to appreciate the food as we eat it, we can reply that the art of food is not an art with that degree of complexity: its works of art are not as complex as a complex piece of music, such as a symphony, in which the composer may introduce into the last movement references to themes played in earlier movements. We might also make the point that, whatever may be said about food, most people's memory for music is in any case limited; the average listener – unless he has heard the work several times – cannot pick up references to the beginning of a work at the end of it. And if some feature requiring memory for its appreciation was untypically introduced into a work of art based on food, it seems likely that the expert would be as aware of it as the expert music listener would be of a reference in music – for example, the discerning diner would, like the expert listener, pick up the reference if a flavour in the savoury recalled a note, as people say, in the *hors d'œuvres.*

If, on the other hand, the claim is that memory is needed for subsequent analysis, the observation would show not that there can be no food art, but that there can be no food criticism. In fact those who write critically about food, such as food correspondents in newspapers or *Good Food Guide* inspectors, seem to be able to recall the food with as much precision as the subject-matter requires – aided no doubt by written notes, as any kind of critic might be.

I turn now to the arguments about the limitations of tastes themselves. The tenor of my reply is similar to that concerning our limitations. As before, I would say both that the claims are exaggerated and that the kinds of art which are used as the touchstone are particularly complex.

First, the regular patterns: it is said that tastes do not have an inherent sequence as colours or musical pitches do, so they cannot be arranged in 'systematic, repeatable, regular combinations' (Beardsley 1958: 99). But it is not true that there are no sequences in tastes. We can arrange them in sequence from sweet to sour, for example, or from least salty to most salty. And not all art forms have 'systematic, repeatable, regular combinations': this is true of music and architecture, but not of representative painting or sculpture. In any case, food does allow of systematic, repeatable, regular combinations: the cook creates the possibility for them, which the eater then realises. Suppose a diner eats in rotation mouthfuls of: duck in orange sauce; new potatoes with cream and garlic; broccoli. Is this not a systematic, repeatable, regular combination? It will be varied now and again by the introduction of mouthfuls of wine, but this does not make it indiscernible.

The second argument, the one concerning form, is that food does not allow a combination of features, as in a face or a tune; that such a combination is necessary for form (meaning something like 'structure'); and that form is necessary for beauty. It is said that a chord in music, for example, is unlike a combination of flavours. A chord in music has both form (in the spacing of the pitch of the notes) and timbre (the characteristic quality of the sounds produced by the musical instrument or instruments), but flavours have only something analogous to timbre (Gurney 1880: 243–4).

This argument is puzzling. First of all, it does not seem to be true that form is required for beauty: we can say that the blue of the sky or the sound of one note on an oboe is beautiful. Perhaps the claim should be that form is required for the complexity which is involved in an art. Second, it is not clear why we may not say that some combinations of tastes have form. Take, for example, a salty biscuit, spread with unsalted butter, and topped by a very bland cheese with an anchovy or olive. Here the four elements can be arranged in order of saltiness, somewhat like a chord with notes of four different pitches. And since each of these four elements tastes of more than just salt, there is another dimension of variation, analogous to the timbre which is also present in a chord. We could also arrange the four elements according to the solidity of their texture, from the butter to the biscuit. I would not claim that form in food can be as complex as in music – for one thing the dimension of time has nothing like the impact that it has in music. But it would be a mistake to say that form is lacking altogether.

It is also claimed that tastes do not allow such things as balance and climax. I can only suppose that those who say that balance and climax are not possible in food have never planned a menu for a dinner party. Certainly a cook planning a dinner, or indeed a discerning diner choosing his meal in a restaurant, thinks partly in terms of these things. For example, he does not put the most striking dish at the beginning, leaving the rest to be an anticlimax. He will accompany elaborate dishes with simpler ones, so that attention does not get dissipated, and so on. Margaret Visser, in *Much Depends on Dinner*, conveys this point well:

> A meal is an artistic social construct, ordering the foodstuffs which comprise it into a complex dramatic whole, as a play organises actions and words into component parts such as acts, scenes, speeches, dialogues, entrances, and exits, all in the sequences designed for them. However humble it may be, a meal has a definite plot, the intention of which is to intrigue, stimulate, and satisfy.

(Visser 1989: 14–15)

I conclude that there are no limitations, in us or in the nature of tastes themselves, which prevent food from giving rise to works of art in the evaluative sense of that phrase, though these will be simpler than in the arts of sight and sound.

IMPLICATIONS OF FOOD AS AN ART FORM

Why does all this matter? If food at its best deserves to be treated as a simple art form, as I have suggested, what follows?

We think of the arts as an important part of our lives. In our society, this manifests itself in at least three ways. The state spends some of its resources on support for the arts; educationalists try to inculcate some knowledge of and concern for the arts into their pupils; and individuals cultivate the arts, and regard someone with no respect for them as defective, a philistine. Should the art of food find its place in all these activities?

There are certainly people who feel that one should cultivate the art of food, eat elegantly and discerningly, 'take trouble' with one's food. They regard this as part of being civilised, and hold that a person who thinks that it does not matter what one eats is at best boorish. But even if we agree that everyone should cultivate the arts, does it follow that everyone should cultivate this particular art? There are at least two reasons why we should not conclude this. First, a person cannot appreciate any art form unless it means something to him or her. It may not therefore be possible for everyone to cultivate every art, and so we cannot prescribe that everyone must cultivate one particular art form. Second, given that time and resources are limited, an individual has to choose from among the art forms that he can appreciate, and the kind of art form that food is will affect that choice. I shall argue in the next section that food represents not only a simple but also a minor art form. If this conclusion is granted for the moment, others follow. For example, it would be reasonable for a person without much time or money to decide, while fully aware of the aesthetic claims of food, that for him major arts had to come first and that food could not be an art form in his life.

Whether such a decision is reasonable partly turns on how expensive good food is; and we can now see the relevance of state subsidy. If fine restaurants were subsidised sufficiently, no one would need to reject this art form merely on grounds of cost. In fact they are not subsidised at all. Is this misguided of the state? I think we can say that it is not, for two reasons, both depending on the fact that money is limited. First, given that a choice has to be made, it is appropriate to subsidise the major arts rather than the minor ones. And second, this particular art form will survive without subsidy. With some arts, such as opera, the point of subsidy in Britain seems to be not to enable everyone to afford to share in an art form, but to prevent it from disappearing altogether. On that criterion there is no need to subsidise good restaurants.

The third way in which the importance of the arts is recognised is in the role they have in education. Teachers try to initiate their pupils into at least the rudiments of an understanding of the major arts. This would not commonly be extended to the art of food, except perhaps for those in domestic science classes. Again the problem is one of priorities: given that time and resources are limited, it seems more important to tell children about the major arts. But this decision may be short-sighted. The advantage of food from the teacher's point of view is precisely the feature which might seem to make it a disadvantage aesthetically speaking: namely, that everyone has to eat. With food, as with clothes, people have a chance to enhance an area of their everyday lives. So to that extent the aesthetic appreciation of food is not a separate, alien activity, but an aspect of what is done every day.

The universality of eating might make some argue that there cannot be an art of food: appreciation of the arts requires a cultivated understanding, but everyone eats, so there cannot be an art of food. It will by now be clear that this argument is confused. Not all eating is an aesthetic activity. Aesthetic eating, if I may call it this, is eating with attention and discernment food which repays attention and discernment. And to achieve attention and discernment may well take some practice and some instruction. On the other hand, the art of food is easier to appreciate than arts which require a lot of background information; the art of food is a possible people's art.

A MINOR ART

I must now make good my promise to show that the art of food is not only a simple art but also a minor one. At first I thought that a simple art was necessarily also minor: my argument was that something complex can support a more sustained aesthetic contemplation than something which is simple, and is therefore aesthetically more satisfying. This argument is sound if the contemplation is of an analytical kind. But there also seems to be a non-analytical kind of aesthetic contemplation, which can be sustained even when it has a simple object such as an abstract sculpture of simple shape. I therefore cannot assume that the art of food is a minor art merely on the ground that it is simple.

It might plausibly be claimed, however, that the art of food is minor because it is not only simple but also limited in three important ways: food is necessarily transient, it cannot have meaning and it cannot move us. I shall look briefly at each of these three claims.

There are two reasons why transience might make a work of art less important. One is that it limits the contemplation that is possible – a work of food art will not be around very long to be contemplated. The other reason is that transient works of art cannot acquire the stature that a long-lived work of art can have. To be a great work of art, an object must have had the chance to 'speak' to different generations, as for example the Taj Mahal and the *Odyssey* have. This limitation – the inability to speak to different generations – affects food in two ways.

We have seen that in the sphere of food there are two kinds of work of art: the recipe, analogous to a musical composition, and the dish as cooked on a particular occasion, analogous to a performance. Now a recipe is not transient, because it can be written down, but despite its permanence, it may still not be able to speak to different generations, not because it is impossible to note down everything with sufficient precision – the cook can interpret, as we said – but because the nature of ingredients changes: for example, farmers breed leaner animals for meat nowadays in response to modern worries about cholesterol, and varieties of fruit and vegetables are constantly changing. Performances, however, are transient. It is true that we can now record most kinds of performance, and that some performances may as a result gather the stature of permanent works of art. But a dish of food is more transient than other kinds of performance, because we cannot reliably record the performance of a cook. I do not only mean that we do not yet have the technology, though that is true; food loses its taste eventually, whatever means we use to preserve it. I also mean that there is a highly relevant reason why we may not be able to record a genuine cookery performance, one intended for particular eaters: if the food is any good, they will eat it all!

We must conclude that works of art in food, whether creative or interpretative, cannot gain the same stature as those of greater permanence. This is one important reason why food must remain a relatively minor art. We might say the same, for the same reason, about any art of the short-lived kind – an art of fireworks, for example, or of flower arranging. The peculiar poignancy of fireworks and flowers depends on their evanescence, and such art cannot have immortality as well.

The second claim, that food cannot have meaning, needs a word of explanation, since in Chapter 2 I mentioned many ways in which food does have meaning: for example, it can symbolise a nation's way of life and traditions. However, what I am about to show is that it does not have the same kinds of meaning as the major art forms have.

To begin with, food does not represent anything else, as most literature and much visual art does. We can see the representational arts painting and literature as telling us something about the world and ourselves, and we can see the world and ourselves in the light of ways in which they have been depicted in the representational arts. But we cannot do either of these things with food. This is an important way in which some of the arts have meanings which food cannot have.

However, it might be said with justice that an art does not need to be representational in order to be a major art. Music, for example, does not represent the world so much as create another world of its own. In that respect the art of food might be said to resemble music: it creates its own world of tastes and smells. But music, although it is not in general representational, seems to be able to carry another kind of meaning, one of which food is not capable: music can express emotion. There is a philosophical problem about what it means to say that music expresses emotion, as well as a problem about how music does it, but it is at any rate clear that it does, and that food does not. And it is important to us that music expresses emotion: it is one of the things that is meant by the claim that music is a kind of communication.

The inability of food to express emotion does not mean that cooks cannot express themselves in their work. For one thing, 'expressing oneself' need not mean expressing emotion. Since cooking gives scope for taste, inventiveness and discernment, cooks can express these qualities through their cookery. For another thing, cooking can in one sense be an expression of emotion. A cook can cook as an act of love, as we have seen, or out of the joy of living. But whereas in music the emotion is somehow expressed in the product itself – the music can be sad or joyful, angry or despairing – in food the emotion is only the motive behind the product.

Lastly, food cannot move us in the way that music and the other major arts can. This claim is different from the claim that food cannot express emotion. A great building, for example, can move us without itself expressing emotion; so can some kinds of music. But is it true that food cannot move us? Speaking for myself, I should say that good food can elate us, invigorate us, startle us, excite us, cheer us with a kind of warmth and joy, but cannot shake us fundamentally in that way of which the symptoms are tears or a sensation almost of fear. We are not in awe of good food, and we hesitate to ascribe the word 'beauty' to it, however fine it is. (Of course, we often say that a dish is beautiful. But that means much less. All kinds of things can be called beautiful, but very few kinds of thing can be said to have beauty, still less great beauty.) If I am right about the absence of this earth-shaking quality in the art of food, it constitutes a limit to the significance it can have for us.

If food cannot be more than a minor art form, there is a danger of being precious about it – of treating it, that is, as though it had more aesthetic importance than it does. So although food may be an art form, we should not always treat it as such. For one thing, not all food constitutes a work of art. If we carefully contemplate every meal with an eye to balance and climax, harmony and contrast and so on, not only will we often be disappointed in our aesthetic aspirations, but also we will fail to get the pleasure that we could get, both from the food and from the other aspects of the occasion. And even on an occasion where the food repays aesthetic study, we may spoil its appeal by too close a scrutiny, like someone looking for Schubertian profundity in a folk song, and also pay so much attention to it that we miss other aspects of the occasion.

This is a subtle matter. Even with Schubert, we can spoil the experience by telling ourselves, 'This is art', instead of letting the song speak for itself. With the art of food, we have two problems. We need to strike a balance between the aesthetic claims of the food on a particular occasion and the social claims of that occasion. We also need to find a middle way between two unsatisfactory attitudes to the aesthetic dimension of food: we must not be so heedless as to waste a satisfying kind of aesthetic experience, but not so precious as to expect more of it than it can give.

4   Food duties

DUTIES TO OTHERS; TO OURSELVES; TO ANIMALS

This chapter is in three parts. First, I deal with issues arising from our duties to other people concerning food. The two most important food-related duties to others, namely our duty to help the hungry and the duties that arise from hospitality, are discussed in Chapter 1 and Chapter 5 respectively; this chapter deals with the rest. Then I consider food duties to ourselves, and more specifically the part played by food in pursuing ideals and the worthwhile life, which is an important theme in this book. Finally, I consider our duties to animals in the sphere of food. This last part is itself in three subsections: a review of some prohibitions on food that do not seem to have a basis in morality; a defence of vegetarianism; and an evaluation of some common objections to vegetarianism. The thesis that we have a duty to refrain from eating meat seems to me one of the most important moral issues concerning food, second in importance only to our duty to help the hungry.

DUTIES TO OTHERS CONCERNING FOOD

Some duties are universal, either in the sense that they fall upon everybody, or in the sense that they are owed to everybody. A duty which is both is the duty not to kill or restrict the liberty of others, which corresponds to other people's human right not to be killed or have their liberty restricted. But most duties are not universal – they are owed by specific individuals or groups to other specific individuals or groups. Such specific duties arise either from contracts and promises, or by virtue of a personal relationship between the duty-owner and the right-holder. Duties regarding food are found in all three categories – universal, contractual and personal.

Some people claim that they have no duties to others; they no longer work, and so have no contractual duties, and they have no family and so no duties of relationship. But it is not so easy to escape from duties to others. Apart from the duty to help one's community in some way, there is for example the duty to be courteous to those whom one meets. So the claim to have no duties to others must be met with scepticism.

To deal with universal duties first, everybody has one duty to others concerning food, and that is the duty to eat healthily. This is one aspect of a more general duty to look after one's own health. Many people would say either that we have no duty to look after our own health, or that if we do it is a duty we owe to ourselves but not to others. I contend, however, that since we all have duties to others, and since our state of health has a considerable bearing on how well we perform them, we all have a derived duty to others to look after our health: to eat healthily, take adequate exercise and get enough sleep. Since this duty is a derived duty, it is owed not to everybody, but to everybody to whom one has a duty. But since there are universal duties, that comes to the same thing.

Those who have contractual duties to others in the sphere of food are the professional providers of food: farmers, fishermen, market-gardeners, food retailers, restaurateurs, caterers, professional cooks, and so on. While these providers have legal contracts with their customers, most people would hold that they also have moral obligations, arising out of these contracts, to sell them food of good quality. What I mean is that, if they sell bad food, they are not only liable to legal action, but are also thought to have broken a moral undertaking. The evidence for this is that if someone negligently or fraudulently provided bad food, but escaped legal action on a technicality, we would not think that he was thereby morally exonerated.

Some commentators deny that contracts give rise to any moral obligations. They claim that in any commercial relationship it is the customer's responsibility to look at what he is getting, and that if he buys poor goods he has only himself to blame. This is the doctrine of 'caveat emptor' or 'let the buyer beware'.

'Caveat emptor' as a general doctrine can be demolished quite quickly. First, the buyer cannot beware unless he can inspect the goods: but many goods – quite apart from those sold by mail-order or direct from showcases – are too heavily packaged to allow inspection. Second, the buyer needs to know something about the goods, but with many purchases this is an absurd suggestion. How many of us could tell by examining it whether a clock, a kitchen-knife, a personal computer was a well-made piece of merchandise? Third, there may be no goods to inspect – either because they do not exist when the contract is made, as with bespoke tailoring, or because they are intangible, as with consultancy. And finally, it is not clear that 'caveat emptor' does in fact remove moral responsibility from the seller. Many sellers at any rate do not follow it – they offer advice about their goods, and will dissuade a buyer from making a purchase that they think is not in his interest. They may of course do this simply because it is in their own interest not to have a disgruntled customer, but many people believe that it is the honest and reputable way to behave.

The result is that, if 'caveat emptor' is to mean anything at all, it has to be put in a somewhat looser form – that the purchaser buys on price and reputation, for example. Then if the cheap apples from the vanishing trader turn out to be maggoty, he has no grievance. But equally this looser form of the doctrine lays upon the trader a moral obligation to live up to his reputation, since that was the thing that the buyer inspected.

The limitations of 'caveat emptor' are particularly pertinent to the food industry. Virtually all the food we buy to cook ourselves is – for good reason – packaged and so cannot be examined; even vegetables are sometimes bagged and sealed so that they cannot be touched. Nor do ordinary people have the skill to judge: raw food can appear fresher than it is as the result of techniques of preservation, and manufactured food may include unexpected additives and colourings. Reputable sellers of food do now provide information about sell-by dates, additives, and so on. But their aim in doing this is not to bring back the doctrine of 'caveat emptor' – that would not be consistent with the policy which they also adopt of immediately refunding any unsatisfactory purchase; rather they aim to increase their reputation by claiming that the customer can now make an informed choice.

As regards the food we do not cook ourselves – the food we buy, that is, in restaurants and take-aways – that clearly falls into the category of goods that cannot be inspected until the contract has been fulfilled. There is a further problem in that a judgment may be slow in forming. I remember the diner at the next table to mine in a well-known Scottish hotel, who was finding his salmon unpalatable. At the end of the meal, when asked, he said he hadn't enjoyed it, and the restaurateur took offence at this: 'Well, you ate it, didn't you?' she cried, and flounced off in a huff. One could sympathise in retrospect with the diner's growing realisation not only that the fish was dry and tasteless, but also that he had eaten too much of it to send it back.

Not all of the duties to others that are incumbent on purveyors of food are contractual duties, arising simply out of their contracts with their customers. Food providers belong to the small group of trades and professions that sell, by way of day-to-day routine, goods that can seriously harm people; electricians and toy-sellers are others in the same group. So a food supplier's duty not to kill or damage people by supplying contaminated food, for example, is too important to be thought of as simply contractual (and still less as adequately removed by 'caveat emptor'). It is better seen as an instance of a universal duty – a duty owed to everyone in respect of their human right to life and freedom from injury.

Duties to others in the sphere of food arise not only out of obligations to people at large and out of contracts, but also out of personal relationships. One such relationship is the relationship between host and guest, which I shall discuss in the next chapter; another is the relationship between spouses. Let us take the case where there are children that one spouse or partner has to stay at home and look after, since that focuses the arguments rather sharply.

The question of who stays at home and looks after the children is what feminists call a gender issue: part of the wider question of whether men and women have inherently different roles. People tend to think, even after thirty years of feminist debate, that it is appropriate for the woman to look after the children, because – they say – women have a natural instinct for nurturing others. There was a time when feminists would reject this claim on the grounds that what is said to be an instinct is in fact the result of social conditioning. Recently, however, there has been a reaction in favour of the view that women may be innately more disposed than men to care about individuals in what may be called personal and nurturing ways (Midgley and Hughes 1983: 185–215). Carol Gilligan's famous work on the difference between men's and women's conception of morality, *In A Different Voice* (Gilligan 1982), supports that view: she finds that women think of morality in terms of caring and responsibilities, men in terms of fairness and rights.

The result of these changes in the climate of opinion is that a woman who has a feeling that she ought to be the one to stay at home does not know what this feeling represents – is it her innate nurturing instinct, a genuine and typically female moral insight about the importance of care, or a piece of social conditioning? But in the end it makes no difference. In the first place, none of these considerations actually entails that the obligation rests on her, rather than on her man: we are entitled to resist instincts and conditioning, and Gilligan's findings show not that women should do all the caring, but only that they set greater store by it than men do. And in the second place, whatever this feeling is deemed to represent, a woman is still entitled to follow its promptings and not waste energy swimming against the psychological tide. A decision to do this would only be wrong if, on the one hand, she pretended that she had no choice, or if, on the other, there were factors in play that were not gender issues at all – perhaps her work is important to society and his is not, or perhaps he too has an instinct to nurture others. And if their claims are equally well-founded, no doubt they can draw lots!

This may all seem a long way from food. But the same questions of gender arise over dividing up the domestic tasks: should all the cooking and housework fall to the woman, for example, and all the household maintenance and gardening to the man? And of course the same answers apply: either party is entitled to follow their feelings, provided they do not pretend that they have no choice and provided that there are no overriding external considerations. Of course, a woman would be wise to make sure that the decision did not lead to her exploitation – an instinct to nurture is one thing, doing all the washing-up as well as all the cooking quite another.

DUTIES TO OURSELVES CONCERNING FOOD

I now wish to show that we have duties to ourselves concerning food. I shall argue that we have duties to ourselves; that these duties consist in exercising our autonomy and promoting our self-development; that the exercise of autonomy and the promotion of self-development consist in the pursuit of ideals; and that all ideals entail instrumental duties concerning food (that is, duties which are not part of the ideal, but are necessary for its realisation), while many concern food more directly.

However, I must first deal briefly with the claim that duties to oneself do not make sense. There are two reasons why this claim might be made. One is based on a view about the nature and basis of morality, and the other on the proposition that there are no corresponding rights.

It is sometimes claimed that morality is essentially about interpersonal relationships – it is a system of rules which ensures that people treat others as well as they treat themselves, or it is a social contract whereby we agree to behave properly to other people provided they agree to do the same to us. On this view there cannot be duties to oneself, since one's relationship with oneself is not governed by a system of rules or a social contract. However, there is no need to see morality in this way: it can also be seen as a set of beliefs, many of which no doubt concern duties to others, but which taken as a whole lay down how we ought to live in general. And the moral self's relationship with itself, in the form of conscience, is a theme of philosophy that stretches back as far as Socrates.

The second argument for the claim that there cannot be duties to oneself is that duties are binding on us whether we like it or not, and duties to ourselves could not be, because no one can exact them. If this means that no one can impose them by threat of sanctions, the same is true of some duties to others, such as the duty to be courteous, so the argument cannot show that there are no duties to ourselves. If, however, it means that no one can exhort us to fulfil them, this does not match our everyday experience: other people certainly disapprove if we neglect such duties, and sometimes express their disapproval, so they at least believe that such duties exist. A more focused form of the argument starts with the assumption that rights may always be waived if the right-holder chooses. If I have a duty to someone else, I am bound to perform that duty unless the other party, the person who has a right against me to have the duty performed, chooses to waive the right. If I have a duty to myself, it is said, this entails that I have a right against myself, but since rights can always be waived, I can choose to waive my right against myself and so release myself from the duty.

This more focused form of the argument is not cogent because the premise is false: we are not always morally entitled to waive our rights. For example, I am surely not morally entitled to waive my right not to be enslaved or my right to education. Not only do we disapprove of someone who robs another person of liberty or education, we also disapprove of anyone who acquiesces in being robbed of these things. To put it another way, we think of the rights to liberty and education as so important that people may not release either themselves or others from respecting them.

However, some people have more freedom of action as slaves than they would as free persons, and similarly some people get more out of foreign travel than they would out of education. So these people seem to be justified in waiving their right to liberty or education. But this is not really the case: what they have waived is their right to one specific form of liberty or education, in order to benefit from a different form of it. What these cases show is not that we have no obligations to ourselves in this area, but rather that our obligations concern broad, vague values that can be realised in more than one way. What we ought to seek is not simple liberty, but the freedom to direct ourselves instead of being directed by others; not simple education, but the chance to make the most of ourselves and our talents. In other words, what we ought to seek is the opportunity to pursue the wider and less specific values which philosophers call autonomy and self-development.

So my claim is that, as well as respecting the autonomy and self-development of others, we have obligations to pursue our own. Our duty to respect these things in others is not controversial; it is the notion of a similar duty to ourselves that is contentious. But two considerations support this claim. The first is that we do in practice believe in such duties to ourselves: we disapprove of people who have no self-respect or independence, or who do not make the most of themselves, and we are ashamed if we detect these traits in ourselves. The second consideration is that it does not make sense to believe in a duty to respect others' autonomy but not in a duty to respect one's own. I am not only saying that if these things matter in other people they must matter in oneself, though I think that is true. I am saying that a duty to respect others' autonomy and self-development is pointless unless they conceive of themselves as having a duty to respect their own.

It is primarily the individual that fosters his or her own autonomy and self-development – these are not activities that other people can undertake for us. Moreover, autonomy and self-development are intimately bound up together in the personal life, because one way in which we develop ourselves is by the process of making choices. The choices that we make reflect in turn the insights, talents, personality and character that we develop; in other words, the exercise of autonomy and the pursuit of self-development reinforce each other. Given that it is only the individual concerned that can be responsible for this process, to say that I have a duty to respect others' autonomy and self-development, but that they do not have a duty to respect their own, does not make sense.

The notions of autonomy and self-development can be analysed further in terms of the notion of ideals. I have said that exercising autonomy, the process of choosing, is itself one way of developing ourselves. But choosing only does this because we choose things for reasons, we choose them because they seem worth having. Where obligations to others are not concerned, the reason for a choice might simply be that it is enjoyable. But if we have a duty of self-development, we ought also to choose pursuits because they enable us to make the most of ourselves by cultivating our talents and gifts. However, most people have many different talents and gifts, not all of which can be developed, so a further choice of which talents to develop is called for. People may make this choice for various reasons, but since developing one's talents is developing oneself, the real point at issue in the choice is: what kind of person do I want to be? So the choice is the choice of an ideal, or ideals, of life: a kind of picture in the light of which individuals model their personal lives.

Pursuing an ideal may mean more than cultivating some of the talents which belong to it. It may also involve pursuing worthwhile experiences and activities, which may incidentally develop the personality but which are not valued for that reason. For example, a person who pursued an artistic ideal might think he should go to see works of art, not because this would be good for his self-development, but because this activity was a part of the way of life his ideal enjoined. In other words, the choice of ideals entails the choice of a particular kind of worthwhile life, in which the chooser expresses the ideals both in what he becomes and in what he does.

But does it make sense to say that we have a duty to follow something – an ideal – which we have chosen for ourselves? Surely a duty is something laid upon us, but a choice is a choice? It does make sense: it is not inconsistent to say that we have a duty to commit ourselves to an ideal or ideals, but a choice as to which ideals. What we have a duty not to do is to drift along not trying to be or do anything in particular.

Are there limits on what can count as an ideal, or a piece of self-development? John Stuart Mill, in claiming that the process of choosing how to spend one's life is itself a process of self-development, implies that it is the choosing that counts, rather than what is chosen (Mill 1962b: 184–93). By self-development, however, Mill meant development of the 'distinctive endowment of a human being', the 'human faculties of perception, judgment, discriminative feeling, mental activity, and even moral preference', and, given his doctrines on the higher and lower pleasures, it is clear that he would have insisted that what is chosen should cultivate this distinctive human endowment (Downie 1966).

We may think Mill's view unduly narrow – for example, as I argued in Chapter 2, we ought not to think of the self as simply the mental. But there are evidently limits. What are we to make, for example, of a person who spends all his spare time developing larger and ever larger muscles? It is certainly self-development – of a kind – but can it really be part of an ideal of life? Most people would think that it cannot, but it is difficult to demonstrate that it is not, and to dismiss the objection that body-building is just as worthwhile for the body-builder as composing symphonies is for the composer. One might, however, ask the body-builder whether, looking back on his life later, he will think that he has made the most of it, and the most of himself. And if he says he will, he is clearly beyond personal reconstruction.

The thesis that we have a duty to pursue ideals will not convince everybody. Surely, some will object, we pursue ideals not out of a sense of duty, but because of the joy, interest, nobility and glamour of the ideal itself? Moreover we approve of this in others: what we admire about those who devote themselves to an ideal is that they are caught up whole-heartedly in what they do, in a way that is not characteristic of duty (Wolf 1982). It is true that we think like this, but the fact that we pursue ideals other than from a sense of duty does not entail that we have no duty to pursue them. And in fact we do pursue ideals out of a sense of duty as well as out of a sense of joy. Not in the detail of daily life, admittedly, but in more reflective moments responsible people will consider not only whether they are fulfilling what they owe to others, but also whether they are making the most of themselves and their lives, in ways of their own choosing.

If I choose an ideal because it embodies a worthwhile way of life, that might seem to commit me to believing that everybody should follow that ideal and do the same as I do. There are people who think like this, but we call them fanatics (Hare 1963: 157–85). It is in fact perfectly coherent to maintain that there are different styles of good life, each of which is equally worthwhile, and that each individual is entitled to choose which of these to pursue. The styles must of course be compatible – a person who is keen on physical fitness, for example, would have difficulty in reconciling the pursuit of that ideal with the pursuit of gourmet excellence (Hare 1963: 155).

I have argued that we have a duty to ourselves to pursue an ideal or ideals. Two questions now arise. First, how is this duty related to food? And second, can we draw any general conclusions about the role of food in the pursuit of ideals, if different people have different ideals?

The second question can be answered by pointing out that the pursuit of any ideal, whatever it may be, requires a proper approach to food. I have already argued that we all have a duty to eat healthily in order to carry out our duties to others; it is equally true that we all have a duty to eat healthily in order to be able to carry out our duties to ourselves. Since this duty to be healthy is derived from other duties to ourselves, it goes no further than what is needed to enable each individual to pursue his or her particular ideals. For example, if I have chosen an intellectual ideal, I have a duty not to get so overweight that I cannot get up the stairs to my study; but I do not have a duty to remain slim enough to be able to wear elegant clothes, unless I also have an ideal of elegance. But though this duty to eat healthily is limited, it still means that food plays a part in the pursuit of any ideal.

However, an individual may pursue excellent health as an ideal in its own right, and this ideal would clearly involve a higher standard of health than is required for the pursuit of most other ideals. We can see the pursuit of such an ideal as a celebration of what the body at its best can be, or as the development of a personal gift which it would be wrong to waste. In the same way people pursue ideals of physical strength and skill, or physical beauty. Such ideals are of course open to the charge that they can become obsessions, and are not then autonomously chosen. But it does not follow that there is no such thing as self-chosen ideals of this kind, and they all have implications for their devotees' choice of food which go beyond what is necessary for maintaining the level of health which is required for all pursuits.

So far the connection between food and ideals which I have described is rather indirect. I have mentioned the general duty to oneself to eat as healthily as is necessary for the pursuit of one's particular ideals, and noted that the pursuit of some particular physical ideals requires healthy eating. But many ideals involve food much more directly and centrally than this. If my ideal is hospitableness, or friendship, or excellence in family life, food and eating can form an important part of the pursuit of these ideals. If I choose the artistic way of life as an ideal, having interesting food can form part of this ideal, because food can constitute an art form, as we saw in Chapter 3. If I choose an ideal of style and elegance, having stylish and elegant food will be part of my quest to make life stylish and elegant. If I have as an ideal a life which is in tune with nature and the environment, I will need to eat food which is organically grown, and perhaps grow some of it myself.

As with any ideal, the pursuit of ideals related to food requires the exercise of autonomy, both in choosing the ideal in the first place, and in deciding how to realise it. People with ideals develop themselves not only through these choices and decisions, but also by developing specific talents. One such talent, when the ideal concerns food, is the cultivation of taste and discernment in food, so that they can choose it for themselves and others in a way that is in accordance with their ideal. Another, of course, is a talent for cookery; not necessary for a wealthy pursuer of an ideal concerned with food, but indispensable to others.

I have depicted our duties to ourselves as the pursuit of one or more ideals of life. I hope also to have shown that food plays an integral role in many of these ideals and an instrumental role – one which does not form part of the ideal, but is a necessary means to its realisation – in the pursuit of all ideals.

NON-MORAL PROHIBITIONS ON FOOD

Are we morally entitled to eat anything we like? This is not a straightforward question, because although certain foods are prohibited in certain societies, it is by no means clear that these prohibitions rest on moral grounds. Let us therefore examine some of them.

First, there are religious prohibitions, such as the Jewish prohibition of pork. This is not a moral belief in the ordinary sense: if it were, Jews would believe that no one should eat pork. The prohibition rests on the belief that God has forbidden pork to Jews specifically, so the edict is not binding on Gentiles.

The rule can, however, acquire a different significance for non-religious Jews, some of whom keep to the prohibition not out of respect for God's commands, but out of loyalty to the Jewish people and respect for Jewish traditions. But though this practice may be personally commendable and beneficial to the community, it is not necessarily based on a moral belief. It would, however, be based on a moral belief if its practitioner universalised it – that is, claimed that all Jews ought to do the same – and brought the precept under some wider obligation, for example that societies generally, or minority communities particularly, had a duty to preserve the traditions of their forbears.

Second, there is in virtually every society a prohibition against eating human flesh. The prohibition does not simply stem from a belief that it is wrong to kill people for food, because it applies also to those who are already dead. As Cora Diamond puts it, we feel that '*a person is not something to eat*' (Diamond 1978: 468, her emphasis). Our feeling is simply that eating humans is unthinkable, because other human beings are too close to us; Diamond calls eating human beings 'dining on ourselves', and she makes further use of the notion of kinship in discussing why we should not eat animals.

Third, and finally, nobody eats 'vermin' – rats, cockroaches and suchlike. It is not that vermin are merely too disgusting to eat: we think of most insects as too disgusting to eat without classing them as vermin. It is that vermin are somehow beyond the pale, too polluted to eat.

Now this prohibition is in a different category from the others we have looked at. Pork and people are objective things: we know what they are; but what constitutes 'vermin' is whatever a society classifies in that way, and varies from one culture to another. I once read a British housewife's account of her attempt to give her Australian visitors rabbit for dinner – they told her that she might as well have expected them to eat rat. Moreover, the prohibition is irrational, in that it does not depend on the creatures being polluted in the literal sense of carrying dirt or disease or poison. Rabbits are clean, but are vermin to Australians; the Japanese globe-fish (a delicacy of the table) carries a fearful poison but is not vermin. So 'vermin' is a way of saying, in a way that permits no further argument, that there are some creatures which we do not respect.

This suggests that there are also creatures which we do respect, and Cora Diamond spells out the idea more fully:

the notion of vermin makes sense against the background of animals in general as not mere things. Certain groups of animals are then singled out as *not* to be treated fully as the rest are, where the idea might be that the rest are to be hunted only fairly and not meanly poisoned.

(Diamond 1978: 476)

And as we shall see, Diamond thinks that regarding an animal as 'not a mere thing' is still consistent with eating it, though she would want us not to eat it on other grounds.

A DEFENCE OF VEGETARIANISM

Is there anything which it is simply wrong – as distinct from too impious or unthinkable or polluted – to eat? More and more people are coming to think that it is wrong to eat the flesh of animals. (By 'animals' I mean, of course, here and in the rest of this section, non-human animals. Our assumption that 'animals' cannot include 'humans' already suggests that we are biased.) There is now a vast literature on all aspects of morality that concern animals. In this book I shall discuss only the morality of eating them, and only a corner of that large issue. I hope, however, to be able to give the flavour both of philosophical discussions of this topic and of some of the amateur arguments.

I assume that the higher animals at least (mammals and birds, that is) can feel physical pain. To non-philosophers this may seem too obvious to need saying. But many philosophers, old and new, have denied it, usually on grounds connected in some way with the higher animals' alleged lack of language. Their arguments are too complex, and would take us too far into the fields of philosophy of mind and philosophy of language, to discuss here. But since the person in the street, to whom this book is primarily addressed, is not usually sceptical about the possibility of animal pain, let us take it that there is no problem on this point.

If animals can feel pain, one argument against eating meat is that the amount of pain and suffering caused to animals by farming them is greater than the pleasure that humankind gets from eating them. This is certainly true where modern intensive methods are used, though it may not have been the case in traditional societies. It is of course a Utilitarian argument – that we should always do what produces the most pleasure or the least pain. One could object that the reduction in pain and suffering brought about by one individual not eating meat is trivial, but this objection does not meet the argument. The argument is that it is wrong not for one individual to eat meat, but for humans to do so. So each individual has a double duty not to eat meat, first on her own account as a human, and second as part of a campaign that will persuade others to give up the practice. This line of attack – that eating meat causes more pain than pleasure, and that everybody should therefore stop doing it – seems enough to forbid the eating of any animal that has been intensively farmed, if not of those reared by more traditional methods.

Given the difficulty of measuring pain and pleasure in any objective fashion, however, it is impossible to convince a sceptic that the premise of the Utilitarian argument – that the overall pain caused by eating meat is greater than the pleasure – is in fact true. So we might do better arguing instead that it is always wrong to cause needless suffering. Some experiments on animals are no doubt necessary to save human lives, but since we cannot claim that we need to eat meat – at least, not in the developed world – the suffering that farming causes is unnecessary, and eating meat is therefore wrong. This argument also has the merit that its principle, that we should not cause needless suffering, though vague, is more plausible than crude Utilitarianism, which can justify the most frivolous reasons for causing pain if enough pleasure is gained as a result.

But this line of argument still does not justify vegetarianism, because it allows us to eat animals who do not suffer. One way of strengthening it is to claim that keeping animals for food means that they inevitably do suffer. Even if they are kept in pleasant and natural surroundings and killed painlessly, the sudden removal of their young and their companions still finds them capable of missing them and grieving for them, and this kind of suffering is inherent in the process. But a reply to that might be that they can be drugged so that they cease to care.

Now many people, including some who are not troubled by their suffering, find the idea of drugging farm animals distasteful. They feel much the same as people do who are dismayed by tricks with animals in circuses, even though the animal has not necessarily been cruelly treated. The thought is that the creature ought to be treated in ways which respect its normal mode of life and flourishing, in other words its dignity. However, it is not clear that we can say that the animal is wronged by such treatment, if *ex hypothesi* it does not realise what is happening to it. A similar question arises over the sedation of anxious old people: given that they are much happier, even if semi-unconscious, and that they can't understand what is happening, what is wrong with sedating them? Nothing, many people would say, so perhaps drugging farm animals is permissible, and suffering can be avoided, and we can eat the creatures after all.

So let us concede the possibility that animals can sometimes be reared and killed for food without suffering grief – perhaps they can be drugged, or perhaps some species do not mind about their companions. Is there nothing wrong with eating such an animal? In particular, can we say that it has a right to life, and that no matter how pleasantly it has lived, that right is violated by killing it for food?

Some philosophers argue that an animal cannot have a right to life, on the grounds that it is not capable of wanting or valuing such an abstract entity as its life (as distinct from the experiences within it), so life as such does not constitute one of its interests. But this conclusion, as many have observed, does not follow from the premise. John Benson points out (Benson 1978: 533–4) that although an animal may not have the capacity to value its life, its life is still of value to it as long as it is capable of enjoying it. He cites as an example the owner of an ailing pet dog, wondering whether to have it put down on grounds of compassion. The owner would normally consider whether the animal is still capable of enjoying life, and if the answer is yes he will regard himself as bound to keep it alive, despite its becoming a nuisance in the home. This kind of thinking comes naturally to anyone who cares for an animal, and it suggests that we are bound to regard animals as entitled to go on living as long as their experience of life is not painful.

It is tempting to counter these arguments by maintaining that human beings are simply more important than animals, so if humans want to eat animals they are entitled to do so. Of course if this is simply a statement that 'might is right', it has no claim to be a moral defence; at best it is a way of saying that right and wrong do not carry any weight in certain circumstances. But that is not what is usually meant: those who say that human beings are more important usually mean that humans have a special status, and they have this status because they have a soul, or because they are uniquely capable of morality, or language, or reasoning. These considerations can be challenged (for example, on the grounds that the difference between ourselves and animals is one of degree, not of kind), but even if we step round these challenges and grant, for the sake of argument, that human beings are more important than any animal, it does not follow that we are entitled to eat animals. All that follows is that we are entitled to put our preferences first in similar cases.

Consider an analogy. Suppose there is an opinion poll among the readers of a women's magazine about whether children are more important than husbands or vice versa, and there is general agreement that children are more important. This does not mean that a wife should always do exactly what suits the children, whatever the cost to the husband. At most it means that, in cases where the children's and husband's interests are similar and in conflict, the children's interests should take precedence. In every other case the question is what degree of additional importance justifies what degree of privilege. In the case of humans eating animals, however, the interests are not similar: our interest in eating them is a mere preference, but their interest in not being eaten is fundamental. So even if humans are more important, that still does not justify that degree of privilege.

Peter Singer pursues a rigorous discussion of these issues (Singer 1975: 1–27). He concedes that a normal human being may have abilities which make its life more valuable than that of any animal, but this still provides no justification, he argues, for favouring the human being in cases where the animal's interest is the same as the human's. Animal pain – to give an example – is morally as important as human pain, because animals have the same interest as humans in avoiding it, and if we deny this – if we claim, in other words, that an animal's interest in avoiding pain is morally less important than a human being's, simply because it is an animal – then, Singer says, we are showing prejudice in favour of our own species. He calls this prejudice 'speciesism', and for him it is just as unjust as a prejudice in favour of one's own race or sex.

We are guilty of speciesism if we perform on another species an act that we would not perform on a member of our own species who lacked the qualities that would normally differentiate him from the other species. For example, one of the grounds for treating human beings differently from animals – it is alleged – is that human beings have superior capacities; it is this difference that entitles us to carry out scientific experiments on animals. It should follow that we are entitled to carry out experiments on a human being who does not have these capacities (provided of course that what we do will not cause suffering to anybody else). So we could carry out experiments, for example, on severely brain-damaged people who had no parents or relatives to grieve for them. If we disagree, we are guilty of speciesism, because the grounds of our preferential treatment of the humans are not their superior capacities, but simply that they belong to our species.

Singer concludes that we should not inflict on an animal anything which we would think wrong to inflict on a human being who had no more than animal capacities – otherwise we are being unjust and unreasonable in just the same way as the racist or sexist. From this it follows that it is as wrong to eat animals as it would be to eat the mentally handicapped.

Should the meat-eater say that what Singer's arguments show is that it is not wrong to eat the mentally handicapped, and the only thing that prevents us from doing so is a sentimental but ineradicable prejudice? I imagine that no one is prepared to say this. A more plausible strategy for the meat-eater might be to claim is that there is nothing wrong with favouring our own species. For example, Benson argues that to undermine the sense of kinship is to undermine the basis of morality:

That we care at all for strangers of our own species or animals of other species results from our extending to them by sympathy something of the concern that we feel spontaneously for those with whom we have closer connections.... The danger in this attempt to eliminate partial affections is that it may remove the source of all affections.

(Benson 1978: 536)

But even if we concede this claim that we both do and should feel a greater sense of kinship with human beings than we do with animals, nothing seems to follow about the legitimacy of eating animals. All that follows is that, if we must eat one or the other, we should eat animals rather than mentally defective human beings.

However, some philosophers use the notion that kinship is the basis of morality more directly than Benson does, and found upon it another argument against eating animals. This argument – like their cast of mind – is very different from Singer's. In general terms it is that we ought to look upon animals as fellows and kindred, so close to us that it should not occur to us to eat them. This way of looking at animals, these commentators say, is natural – it is the view we hold of our pets – and we can come to have it of other animals too; and they further argue that it is preferable both to Singer's somewhat abstract considerations and to the way in which most people look upon animals in practice. Cora Diamond, for example (Diamond 1978: 473–4), quotes Burns' description of himself to the mouse as 'thy poor earthborn companion, / An' fellow-mortal' and Walter de la Mare's description of a tit at a bird-table as 'This tiny son of life'. Both these descriptions, she says, see the fellowship between creatures as something more than merely biological.

One difficulty with this argument is that we are not obliged to feel kinship. Not everyone thinks of animals as fellow-mortals, and to assume that this is the only sound way of looking at them is to beg the question. But a bigger difficulty, as Diamond herself admits (Diamond 1978: 475), is that the conception of animals as fellow-mortals is still not inconsistent with killing them for food. To think of animals as kin may produce respect; concern; an inability to look upon them as a mere commodity; even a sense that one must treat them well and use humane methods if they are to be killed – but it does not necessarily produce more than this. It does, however, provide a basis on which we can make an appeal: we can ask people who are sympathetic to this idea to go further, and not eat their fellow-mortals if they do not have to.

To summarise, then, we have two rather different types of argument against eating meat. One primarily addresses our notions of reason and justice: if it is wrong to eat any human being, no matter what he or she is like, then it must be unfair and unreasonable to eat those animals which have capacities similar to those of some human beings. The other type of argument addresses our emotions: we feel a kinship with animals, and if this feeling is allowed to blossom it will lead us to conclude that we do not want to eat them. These two approaches involve two different ways of looking not only at the present issue but also at morality in general: one intellectual, one emotional. The intellectual approach is the better strategy for the advocate of vegetarianism to adopt, because in the end feelings do not constitute a valid argument. Readers of Cora Diamond – or of Stephen Clark, who takes a similar line (Clark 1977) – may find that they do not have the feelings ascribed to them, or if they do they may decide that the feelings are sentimental twaddle. They might say, in other words, that people are not obliged to do whatever their feelings prompt them to. But we are obliged to do what a valid argument shows to be right. If the proponent of vegetarianism can demonstrate by argument that eating meat is wrong, then the presence or absence of feelings does not matter, and the right course of action can be followed as a matter of will, as with any other duty.

On the other hand, once the arguments convince one that it is unjust to eat animals, the approach of Cora Diamond and Stephen Clark is more attractive overall. The sense of ourselves as having a kinship with the animals seems a more appropriate attitude to them than detached rationality by itself, just as it does in our attitude to fellow humans, because it corresponds to the fact that we are like them in many ways. How far each of us develops the sense of this kinship is no doubt largely dependent on what encounters we have with animals as individuals – Dick Francis, in one of his novels, describes one such ground-breaking incident, in which the hero is shut in with his terrified racehorse in a horse box which has just been involved in a crash:

> I began to grow interested in him in a way which had not before occurred to me; as a person who happened also to be a horse. I realised I had never before been alone with a horse.
>
> (Francis 1976: 16)

COMMON OBJECTIONS TO VEGETARIANISM

Vegetarians have always had to contend with objections from meat-eaters. Peter Singer's *Animal Liberation* (Singer 1975) and Stephen Clark's *The Moral Status of Animals* (Clark 1977) discuss a great many of these objections. I shall discuss two in particular which I have come across in non-philosophical life, both of which are more penetrating than they at first seem. I shall also deal with some of the inconsistencies of which vegetarians are commonly accused.

The first objection is that since animals eat each other, we are entitled to eat them. It is not clear at first what this objection amounts to – we do not think that we are entitled to do to people everything that they do to others, so why should we be entitled to do it to animals? An alternative version of it, however, is that since animals eat each other they deserve to be eaten themselves.

But that will still not do. In the first place it justifies us in eating only carnivores, and inasmuch as the only carnivores which Westerners regularly eat are fish it does not justify much. Second, fish are incapable of morality – I think everybody would agree with that – and so cannot either deserve or not deserve anything. Third, even if *per impossibile* fish could deserve anything, it does not follow that humans are the ones with the right to mete out the punishment. And fourth, fish cannot live on another diet, whereas human beings can; so fish have a justification on the grounds of self-preservation, but human beings do not.

All these points seem so obvious, and the objection nevertheless so persistent, that one wonders whether there are not more substantial considerations underlying it. I think that there are in fact two. One is the feeling that vegetarianism is mere sentimentality, taking its stand on the rather vacuous claim that Nature is wonderful and we should stay more in tune with her. (Actually what the vegetarian is advocating is something unnatural – that people should refrain from a pleasant, available and wholesome source of food.) The other consideration which I think lies behind the objection also deals with the relationship between human beings and the animal world, but is more precisely focused. It is this: if animals ought not to be eaten, surely we have a duty to prevent carnivorous animals eating others?

Unlike us, however, animals cannot survive without killing other creatures, and it can certainly be argued that we are not entitled to preserve one species at the expense of another (Benson 1978: 547). The implication of this line of thought is that the death of animals for food is not an absolute evil, though it may be one of the less attractive aspects of nature. We can reduce its incidence by refraining from doing it ourselves, but at the same time we can accept its existence in those cases where it is necessary for the preservation of other animals.

The second objection to vegetarianism which I wish to deal with is the claim that, provided they have a reasonably happy life, on balance we benefit animals by rearing them for food. One version of this argument is that many animals reared for food would not exist had we not bred them, and since a short life is better than none we are doing them a favour. This thought does not appear to be coherent, and indeed when I first heard it I thought it was meant as a joke. The favour – according to the argument – is to have brought a being into existence. But how can one confer a favour on a being who does not exist?

If this does not seem convincing, we can use the same manœuvre as Singer used when comparing animals to the mentally handicapped. Suppose a person bred babies for food, and maintained that this was justified because this gave the babies a short life that was better than none – we should think him mad. I do not simply mean that we should think him wicked or insane for thinking that he could breed babies for food: I mean that we should think that his claim to have given them life was irrelevant. And if the argument is cogent for animals but not for human beings, its proponents need to explain why.

As with the objection about animal predators, however, this argument has something more substantial underlying it. Instead of believing that the breeder has earned the right to eat an animal by giving it life, we should consider whether there might not be a hypothetical bargain between the animals and the farmer. In this hypothetical bargain, the animals live more comfortably than in the wild – food and shelter are easier to find, they are protected from diseases and parasites and they die humanely; but they die sooner than they would otherwise, and the occasion of their death is planned and controlled in a way that it would not be if they died naturally or fell to a predator. The bargain is hypothetical because although no individual makes a choice, the price paid for the benefits can still be said to be a reasonable one. The idea is borrowed from the theory of hypothetical contract in political philosophy; according to this theory what makes an arrangement just is not that rational self-interested persons have actually agreed to it, but that they would prefer it to other possibilities (Rawls 1973).

Richard Adams explores a variant of this idea in his novel *Watership Down* (Adams 1973). In this book a group of rabbits who have been forced to flee from their burrow are looking for a new home, and come across a colony of rabbits who have been half-tamed by a farmer. He puts out food for the tamed colony, which they happily eat, and because they do not have to spend so much time foraging they develop a more sophisticated life than the wild rabbits, with poetry and other arts. The price, of course, is that every so often the farmer whisks one of them off to the cooking-pot. In the novel the tame rabbits are depicted as knowing this, but refusing to admit it even to themselves. The visitors flee in horror as soon as they realise what the basis of their hosts' civilisation really is.

It is no doubt possible to read Adams' book as a political and moral allegory. But there is an interesting question about the rabbits' choice, if it is viewed simply as a choice between different possible rabbit ways of life: is it so obvious that the tame rabbits have made the wrong choice? We can leave poetry and art out of the equation; the question is whether a rabbit – or any animal – gets a good bargain when it is domesticated, provided (and it is an important proviso) that it is well treated. It is easy to think, as Adams does, in terms of freedom and proper rabbit life, but these are anthropomorphic concepts. Perhaps the well-treated domestic animal has good reason, from its own point of view, to be contented with such a life, despite the fact that it will die early and not by chance. It is difficult to know whether this is a coherent line of thought, as domestic animals could not survive in the wild in any case. But even if we do decide that notions of proper animal lifestyles are misplaced here, and that an animal would choose such a life if it had the option, this still does not provide a general argument for eating meat: the majority of animals kept for meat are not well treated and do not have good reason to be contented.

Opponents of vegetarianism not only advance objections like those discussed above, they also accuse vegetarians of inconsistency. Since most people fail to live up to their principles some of the time, it is not clear how an accusation of inconsistency counts against any doctrine in general, or vegetarianism in particular; but presumably the point is to show that vegetarians, whether right or wrong, are not entitled to commend their views to others. Alternatively the aim may be to get vegetarians to admit that, since their principle has implications which they find unacceptable, it cannot be justified.

Let us mention first the accusation that for all we know lettuces do not like being cut up, and the like. These attackers are disingenuous, since it would never occur to them to suppose in any other context that lettuces have feelings. But, as so often in this debate, a more serious point lurks behind the facetious one: if it is wrong to kill living things, then vegetarians should not kill plants any more than they should kill animals. Fruitarians hold this view; they live on plants without killing them, by eating the things that fall off the plant, such as fruit and nuts, and not eating things that cannot be eaten without destroying the whole plant, such as carrots. But the majority of vegetarians do not think it wrong to eat something just because it is living. As we have seen, they base their arguments not on whether what they eat was once living or not, but on its capacity to suffer and on our ability to relate to it.

A second inconsistency arises over animal products other than meat – typically milk and its derivatives. Surely, the objectors say, the vegetarian is inconsistent if he drinks or eats these, since the commercial production of milk depends on taking the calf away from its mother and causing suffering (the more so if the calf is then reared for veal). Here ordinary vegetarians have no option but to admit that they are not living up to their principles (Singer 1975: 190–2) – they should use one of the soya milks, as strict vegetarians do. But the indifference of ordinary vegetarians to this issue is interesting. It is as though they were saying that giving up meat is difficult enough – they cannot be expected to give up everything else that might be wrong for the same reasons!

Another form of this argument concerns the wearing of leather, which many vegetarians say they are perfectly happy to do. But the question is how they can rationally and consistently be happy to do it. One suspects that the real problem here is that vegetarian food is chic, whereas plastic shoes are not – and that the shoe manufacturers could alter our perceptions more quickly than philosophers.

Finally, it is alleged that vegetarian hosts who refuse to cook meat for their non-vegetarian guests are being inconsistent: if the non-vegetarian is willing to cook meat-free food for the vegetarian, then the vegetarian – it is claimed – should reciprocate. But though there may be a lack of reciprocity here, there is no inconsistency. The vegetarian thinks it morally wrong to serve meat, whereas the non-vegetarian does not think it wrong to serve vegetarian food, only a nuisance.

However, there is once more another question hiding behind this one, and that is whether it is inconsistent to cook meat if one believes that it is wrong to eat it. Some vegetarians do cook meat for others, and they are subject to a conflict of principles. On the one hand if people think it wrong to eat meat, they are bound to think it wrong to cook and serve it. But they might also think it wrong to give a meat-eating guest less than the best – not what is morally best, but what will give the guest most pleasure.

The case for adopting a vegetarian diet seems to me strong. Indeed, I am struck by the number of people who do not try to argue against it when they meet a vegetarian, but instead say, 'I think you're right – I've been meaning to become a vegetarian, but I haven't managed it yet.' I think that in many cases the explanation for this failure is greed. But that is a topic for Chapter 6.

5   Hospitableness

FOOD AND MORAL VIRTUES

In this chapter and the next I shall discuss two moral virtues which relate particularly to food. The first, hospitableness, is mainly concerned with ways in which its possessors treat other people; the second, temperance, with ways in which its possessors behave with regard to their own eating (though it also has a bearing on their treatment of others). Since temperance is one of the traditional virtues, or at least gluttony is a traditional vice, I shall not spend time in the next chapter arguing that food is a proper sphere for moral virtue concerning oneself; instead I shall try to rescue temperance from rather narrow and negative conceptions of it. With hospitableness the problem is rather different: everyone is agreed that it is an agreeable quality, but it does not seem to be so generally agreed that it is a virtue in its own right. I shall therefore show in this chapter that there is a moral virtue of hospitableness, and discuss what kind of virtue it is.

There are three reasons why the question of whether hospitableness is a moral virtue is philosophically interesting. First, the close link between hospitableness and friendship is relevant to a question that is central in moral philosophy: namely, how far, if at all, morality can be partial and can entitle or oblige us to favour some people over others. Second, the topic of hospitableness raises the question of whether, to be a moral virtue, a trait must be one which everyone should try to acquire. I shall argue that hospitableness (and some other virtues too) are what may be called optional virtues, related to particular choices of how to carry out general moral obligations. Third, the nature of hospitableness challenges our assumption that each moral virtue is based on a specific motivation distinct from the sense of duty. I shall claim that hospitableness is not based on any one motive but derives its distinctive character from the value which hospitable people attach to a particular ideal.

HOSPITALITY

Hospitableness, the trait possessed by hospitable people, is clearly something to do with hospitality, so I shall begin by saying a little about hospitality. We can define hospitality as the giving of food, drink and sometimes accommodation to people who are not regular members of a household. Typically givers, or hosts, provide these things in their own homes, and the point is that they are sharing their own sustenance with their guests. This notion may be stretched in various directions: for example, a firm is said to provide hospitality if it gives food and drink to visitors. But the central idea of the concept remains that of sharing one's own provision with others.

In doing so, a host accepts responsibility for the overall welfare of his or her guests. As the eighteenth-century gourmet and food writer Jean-Anthelme Brillat-Savarin says:

> To entertain a guest is to make yourself responsible for his happiness so long as he is beneath your roof.
>
> (Brillat-Savarin 1970. 14)

If this is a host's task, it is concerned with more than food, and indeed more than food and shelter: it means that a host must try to cheer up a miserable guest, divert a bored one and care for a sick one. Traditionally the most important responsibility of all was for the guest's safety – hospitality was a kind of sanctuary, and the host was thought of as having undertaken a solemn obligation to make sure no harm came to his guest while under his roof. This idea is enshrined in many legends. In Wagner's opera *The Valkyrie*, for example, Hunding the jealous husband cannot kill his enemy Siegmund while Siegmund is his guest – he has to wait until Siegmund leaves and then pursue him. Nonetheless it is food that is of central importance in hospitality, for several reasons.

First, hospitality originally involved meeting travellers' needs in the days before hotels, speedy travel and relatively safe roads. Many different cultures have the belief that strangers and those in trouble and unprotected should be taken in and looked after, and clearly food is an indispensable part of what they need. Nowadays, in a sophisticated and industrialised community, there is not the same need for this aspect of hospitality, but all kinds of emergency can still call upon it, as we shall see.

Second, giving, receiving and sharing food is a symbol of the bond of trust and interdependency set up between host and guest. In some cultures this bond is a permanent one: for example, traditional Bedouin will not fight anyone with whom they have eaten salt (Visser 1989: 67).

Third, giving food is a gesture of friendliness. Any gift can have this role, but several things distinguish food as a gift. One is that its literally vital importance gives it a special symbolic significance. Moreover, hosts try to give their guests particularly agreeable food, thereby pleasing as well as sustaining them; and if they have spent time and trouble making the food themselves, this signifies the generosity of spending time as well as money on the guests. And in sharing food with their guests hosts may also be sharing something else, such as the traditions of their country, region or religion. I discussed some of these meanings of food in Chapter 2.

The nature and importance of hospitality has varied very much in different times and places. But this variation does not mean that there is no trait to discuss. Any trait will manifest itself in ways which differ according to prevailing conditions and conventions. For example, in a society with an institution of duelling, people can be courageous in ways impossible in a society with no such institution. In this discussion of hospitableness I hope to unearth basic concepts which underlie differences such as these.

Brillat-Savarin's translator used the phrase 'entertain a guest' – does this mean the same as 'provide hospitality'? There are contexts in which it is natural to speak of hospitality rather than entertaining, and vice versa: giving a meal to a stranded traveller is hospitality but not entertaining, but giving smart dinner parties seems more like entertaining than hospitality. Where there is a difference, then, hospitality is associated with the meeting of need, entertaining with the giving of pleasure. But this difference is only a matter of nuance. Often the two words are equivalent, and I shall use 'entertaining' to mean the same as 'providing hospitality'.

THE GOOD HOST

The first problem in discussing the good host is a verbal one: should I say 'host or hostess' every time, to make clear that I am referring to either men or women? This would be cumbersome, and I shall therefore adopt the usage that is becoming common with words such as 'actor', 'poet' and 'sculptor', and use the word 'host' to refer to either men or women. Admittedly, this prevents me from using the phrase 'host and hostess' to refer to partners when joint hosts. But it is appropriate in any case to avoid implying that partners are always of different sexes.

Behind the verbal question, however, is another question of more substance. One of the reasons why some female actors do not like to be called 'actresses' is that they do not like the suggestion that what they do is somehow not the same as what a male actor does. But perhaps in the case of hospitality there actually is a difference: does hospitality mean different things to men and to women?

This is a question for psychologists and sociologists rather than philosophers, but we can look at some of the questions they might ask. First, in a traditional household, or in a household in which traditional thinking still lingers, do men and women think of the food they offer to guests as their own in two different senses? For example, the man might think of it as his because he earned the money to buy it, the woman as hers because she prepared it. (Nowadays, of course, both may earn the money for it and both may prepare it, or it may be the woman who earns the money and the man who cooks, so any such division is presumably fading.)

Second, and connected with the first question, are there different ways in which male and female hosts take a pride in being a host? It might be the case, for example, that men tend to be proud of the lavishness of their hospitality, women of the quality of what is offered.

Third, is there any reason to suppose that women have, more so than men, a natural special bent for hospitality? Grounds for such a supposition might be that it constitutes the natural extension of a nurturing instinct, or that it arises naturally from the greater emphasis that women are said to place on personal relationships in their view of morality (Gilligan 1982). The problem with this question, as I said in Chapter 4 in connection with the distribution of duties within the family, is that we cannot discover whether any apparent difference between the inclinations of men and women results from nature or from nurture. However, one can say here, as I said in Chapter 4, that provided she acknowledges that she does indeed have a choice, and provided she does not let herself become exploited, a woman has no reason to resist an inclination to be hospitable merely on the ground that it may be the result of conditioning.

On the other hand, perhaps hospitality, with its possibilities of ritual and formality, is a way in which men can bridge the gap between the rule-bound situations in which they are said to feel at home and more individual relationships and obligations. I leave that question, like the others, to the sociologists and psychologists. In the rest of this chapter I shall write as though men and women can both be hosts, can both be called hosts, and are both moved by the same kinds of thought about hospitality – though there may be other differences which do not matter for our present purpose.

Is hospitableness the same thing as being a good host? This question raises another question, that of what a good host is. One might say that a good host is one who fulfils all the tasks of a host: refills empty glasses, makes sure that guests are offered second helpings, and so on. But any such list cannot describe the essence of a good host, since it applies only to the conventions of a particular time and place. However, we can derive a more general formula from the observation of Brillat-Savarin already quoted. If entertaining a guest is making yourself responsible for his happiness so long as he is beneath your roof, a good host is one who make his guests happy – or as happy as a host's efforts and ministrations can make them – while they are in his care.

Being a good host involves skills as well as effort. Some of these skills, like the tasks of a host, are stereotypes: for example, a good host can prevent a heated argument from becoming a quarrel. If we want a general formula for these skills, it must be this: good hosts are good at making their guests happy. In other words, they know what will please them and are able to bring this about.

Hosts need not include cooking among their skills. They may have a cook, or buy in ready-made food. But if they do not cook themselves, they must have the skill of identifying themselves with the food sufficiently to make it their own gift. There is a difference between saying 'I thought you'd like something refreshing and seasonal, so I've got cook to do a summer pudding with fruit from the garden' and saying 'What is this peculiar-looking thing? Oh well, I dare say it's all right'.

Is being a good host the same as being hospitable? If we say after a party that the host was very hospitable, we may mean no more than that he or she was a good host – skilful and attentive. But being a good host is not really a sufficient condition of being hospitable. For we would say that a host was not being genuinely hospitable if we discovered that he or she had an ulterior motive for being so attentive, one that had nothing to do with any desire to please the guests or any belief in an obligation to do so.

Genuinely hospitable behaviour, then, requires an appropriate motive. However, whether someone should be described as a hospitable person depends on how often hospitable behaviour occurs. One can say, 'She's very hospitable when she entertains, but she almost never does'; such a person is scarcely a hospitable person. A hospitable person, I suggest, is someone who entertains often, attentively and out of motives appropriate to hospitality. (I shall discuss appropriate motives in the next section.)

Being a good host is not even a necessary condition of being hospitable: we can say, 'He is a very hospitable person, but not really a good host'. At first this seems paradoxical: one might think that the motives which prompt genuinely hospitable people to entertain would also prompt them to look after their guests properly. But the paradox disappears when we recall that a good host has to be skilful as well as attentive. Hospitable people are attentive, but they are not necessarily skilful and might be called 'not good hosts' for this reason. Since they genuinely want to please, they will try to overcome their limitations. But not every host, however well-meaning, is as skilful as some hosts who have ulterior motives, just as not all generous people are as good at giving presents as some seducers or confidence tricksters. In any case, eagerness to please brings ineptitudes of its own: hosts who 'try too hard' (who for example urge their guests to have more and more helpings when they have had all they want) embarrass their guests instead of pleasing them.

A good host, then, is not necessarily hospitable; for this an appropriate motive is also required. A person who is frequently hospitable is a hospitable person; he or she will also be a good host so far as attentiveness is concerned, but may lack the skill which would make him or her a good host without qualification.

HOSPITABLE MOTIVES

I have said that if behaviour is to count as genuinely hospitable, it must have an appropriate motive. Let us now consider what motives are appropriate, beginning with a list (which I do not claim is exhaustive) of likely motives for offering hospitality.

First, there is the desire for company, either company in general or that of specific people. Second, there is the desire for the pleasures of entertaining – what we may call the wish to entertain as a pastime. Third, there is the desire to please others, stemming either from general friendliness and benevolence or from affection for particular people. Fourth, there is concern or compassion, the desire to meet another's need. Fifth, there is allegiance to what one considers to be duties: a general duty to be hospitable, a duty to entertain one's friends or a duty to help those in trouble. And finally there are what we may call ulterior motives, those which have nothing to do with the guests' pleasure or welfare.

A common ulterior motive is vanity: a desire to show off something, such as one's culinary skills or sophisticated taste in food. Maggie Lane, in her delightful book *Jane Austen and Food* (Lane 1995), gives some marvellous examples from Jane Austen's novels of hospitality motivated by vanity. Here, for example, is Mrs Elton in *Emma*, fashionable but vulgar, who has just come to the village as a bride, and been entertained by all her new husband's old friends. She is considering how to return this hospitality:

Mrs Bates, Mrs Perry, Mrs Goddard and others, were a good deal behind in knowledge of the world, but *she* would soon show them how every thing ought to be arranged. In the course of the spring she must return their civilities by one very superior party – in which her card tables should be set out with their separate candles and unbroken packs in the true style – and more waiters engaged for the evening than their own establishment could furnish, to carry round the refreshments at exactly the proper hour, and in the proper order.

(Austen 1966: 291)

It is easy to decide that if hosts are moved entirely by ulterior motives they are not being genuinely hospitable; hospitableness must have something to do with concern for the guests. But in practice, of course, motives tend to be mixed. For example, a host may be mainly influenced by a desire to please her guests, but serve a particular dish out of vanity: that is, because she wants to impress them rather than because she wants to please them. She still counts as hospitable if the dominant consideration is the guests' pleasure, but the more she is motivated by the desire to show off her skill or sophistication the less hospitable she is.

Some motivations for offering hospitality (seduction, for example, and other forms of manipulating people through the pleasures of hospitality) are paradoxically both ulterior and dependent on pleasing the guest. Unless the guest is pleased the manipulation does not work, but the host's motivation is still ulterior because he is pleasing the guest only as a means to an end, not for its own sake.

It might be argued that the desire for company should also be classed as ulterior, since it has no essential connection with the pleasure of the guests. However, this motive too tends to be mixed with others. If a lonely person invites people for the sake of their company but is genuinely solicitous of their welfare when they come, he is surely hospitable. But if he spends so much time telling them his troubles that they have to go before he gets round to feeding them, he is clearly not so. What matters in assessing motives for hospitality, then, is not only the initial reason for inviting people, but also what we may call the spirit in which they are entertained, what moves the host when the guests are there. A host can redeem an ulterior motive for an invitation by being concerned for the guests once they arrive.

Is the desire for the pleasure of entertaining an ulterior motive too? After all, it might be argued that hosts who entertain as a pastime are seeking their own pleasure rather than that of the guests. We have to distinguish three possibilities before we can answer this question. First, there are hosts who are essentially indifferent to the pleasure of the guests, since what they enjoy about entertaining – for example, cooking elaborate dishes – does not depend on whether guests enjoy themselves. Such hosts are not hospitable, though if their guests do enjoy themselves, they may either not see this or not think it matters. Second, there are hosts who aim to please their guests without thinking of their own pleasure, and who are pleased when they succeed. Such hosts are clearly hospitable: they are not basically aiming at their own pleasure, and the pleasure they get depends on the success of an activity designed to please others. Indeed, it is the person who does not enjoy entertaining others who might be thought inhospitable, as we shall see.

There is a third possibility, distinct from either of the two just mentioned. Hosts may entertain for their own pleasure, but derive a good deal of that pleasure from feeling that they are pleasing others. I think it is appropriate to call such hosts hospitable, because their hearts are in the right place; they would not get pleasure from pleasing their guests unless they had concern for them. For an example of this kind of attitude to hospitality, consider the following passage from Anna Thomas's *The Vegetarian Epicure*.

> The sharing of food has always been, to me, both a serious and a joyful proposition. Feeding people graciously and lovingly is one of life's simplest pleasures: a most basic way of making life better for someone, at least for a while. Yet, sadly, so few people can find joy in cooking for their friends or family: for men it seems a threat to their masculinity, for women a prison.
>
> I was fortunate in that I seemed always to be surrounded by true hosts. My parents and relatives – old-fashioned Europeans – do not consider entertaining guests or offering refreshment a social chore; rather, it is a pleasant duty, an opportunity to create a little ease. To send a guest away unfed is sacrilege to them. On festive occasions, the banquets which appeared were astonishing.
>
> I delight in the thought that, in our house, friends always feel welcome and always leave refreshed. Sharing food is a large part of this, and whatever the culinary persuasion of my friends may be, I enjoy planning meals for them, preparing the food and serving them myself.
>
> (Thomas 1973: 15)

This passage shows the artificiality of trying to distinguish between entertaining for the pleasure of pleasing one's guests and entertaining one's guests for their sake with pleasure.

In my list of motives for hospitableness I mentioned several kinds of motivation arising from duty. However, there might be doubt about duty as a motive for hospitableness, not because it is ulterior but because it seems to be at odds with the idea of warmth contained in hospitality. If people entertain out of a sense of duty, are they being hospitable or merely dutiful? I suggest that they are being hospitable provided that what I called the spirit of the hospitality is generous. Suppose I am tired of entertaining, but out of a sense of duty invite new neighbours to dinner. If when they come I enter into the spirit of the occasion and want to please them, I am surely being hospitable. But if I continue to feel resentful, I am only being dutiful (though if the neighbours cannot tell the difference, perhaps I am still doing the right thing!)

Hospitable motives, then, are those in which concern for the guests' pleasure and welfare, for its own sake, is predominant. These can include entertaining for pleasure where that pleasure largely depends on knowing that one is pleasing the guests, and sense of duty where there is also concern for the guests themselves. And hospitable people, those who possess the trait of hospitableness, are those who often entertain from one or more of these motives, or from mixed motives in which one of these motives is predominant.

KINDS OF GUEST

We can classify types of hospitality not only by motivation but also by kinds of guest. As we shall see, there is a correspondence between the two classifications, but it is by no means exact. I shall distinguish three kinds of guest: those in a relationship to the host, those in need, and friends proper.

Hospitality to one's circle

Where guest and host stand in a relationship, it can be an official relationship which involves a duty of hospitality (for example, that between students in a university hostel and a warden who is expected to entertain them), or an unofficial connection, such as that between colleagues, neighbours, fellow parishioners, parents whose children are friends, or of course relations – those whom people call their circle. I do not include, in the term 'one's circle', people with whom the only relationship is one of friendship.

I shall not discuss official hospitality at length. A person could not have a trait of hospitableness based only on fulfilling official duties of hospitality, since these duties come and go with a particular post, whereas traits are a long-term disposition. However, officials can carry out official duties of hospitality in the same friendly spirit in which they might entertain those in their circle, and when they are thought of as hospitable it is because they do this. I shall therefore assume that hospitable officials can be regarded as extending their circle to include those they have an official duty to entertain, and not discuss them separately.

Possible motives for entertaining one's circle are enormously varied. One such motive – or ingredient in motivation, for motives can be mixed, as we said – is a sense of duty. In more formal societies, people have strict obligations to entertain, according to their status, others in their circle; these obligations are governed by rules and are no less binding than the warden's obligation in our own society to entertain the students in her hostel. In our own society such rules are largely gone, but we are still apt to feel that entertaining one's circle is a good idea and perhaps a duty. But this sense of duty is not something that applies only when a host has a specific, rule-governed duty to entertain particular guests. People feel that they ought to entertain new neighbours or colleagues, or relations whom they have not seen for a while, on the looser ground that they think that they ought to express solidarity, or strengthen the bonds of family and community, and they see entertaining as a particularly good way of doing this.

Another kind of motive for entertaining one's circle, though hard to characterise, is something like the wish to be friendly, to offer some degree of personal relationship. Entertaining is a good way to be friendly – we noted earlier the role of the gift of food in the offer of friendliness. Entertaining is also friendly for another reason: it involves the offer of a degree of intimacy, a share in the host's home life. This motive can lead people to entertain those with whom their connection is essentially official; it is as if they were saying, 'Let's not be merely business partners, we are human beings as well'. Similarly, the warden might entertain his students 'to show that he is human'.

Where someone frequently entertains his or her circle from one of the hospitable motives I distinguished earlier, he or she is one sort of hospitable person and has one sort of hospitableness. Entertaining one's circle cannot be sharply distinguished either from entertaining those in need or from entertaining one's friends. But there are some points to make about each of these other categories of guest which justify taking them separately.

Good-Samaritan hospitality

I shall give the name 'Good-Samaritan hospitality' to entertaining people simply because they seem to be in need of hospitality. The need might be either a need for food and drink as such, or a psychological need of a kind which can be met particularly well by hospitality, such as loneliness or the need to feel valued as an individual.

Good-Samaritan hospitality can be shown to anyone, whether connected to the host or not. But the clearest cases of it are those where the guest is a stranger and the only reason for offering it is the perception of the guest's need. This kind of hospitality is perhaps the most fundamental kind of all. As I said earlier, in simple communities all travellers are strangers in need of food and shelter simply in virtue of being away from their own home, and there is usually felt to be a corresponding obligation of hospitality. Here, for example, is the swineherd Eumaeus in the *Odyssey* talking to his master Odysseus who has returned home, in disguise, after twenty years. Eumaeus does not recognise him but takes him to be an old beggar.

> 'Sir', said the swineherd Eumaeus, 'my conscience would not let me turn away a stranger in a worse state even than yourself, for strangers and beggars all come in Zeus' name, and a gift from folk like us is none the less welcome for being small.'
>
> (Homer 1946: 222)

The same idea is found in Christian thought:

> Then shall the righteous answer him, saying, Lord, when saw we thee an hungred, and fed thee? or thirsty, and gave thee drink? When saw we thee a stranger, and took thee in? or naked, and clothed thee? Or when saw we thee sick, or in prison, and came unto thee? And the King shall answer and say unto them, Verily I say unto you, Inasmuch as ye have done it unto one of the least of these my brethren, ye have done it unto me.
>
> (*Bible* 1611: Matthew 25, 37–40)

In a modern urban setting, with its hotels and restaurants, strangers do not need hospitality simply because they are strangers. But there is still room for Good-Samaritan hospitality, as is shown by the couple who invited a complete stranger to come for Christmas because they had heard her on the radio talking about her dread of a lonely Christmas after a recent bereavement.

There are many kinds of motivation for Good-Samaritan hospitality, including consciously religious motivation, sense of duty, and loving-kindness, charity, compassion – whatever is the best word for a spontaneous response to those in need. In a particular case it may often not be clear, either to the hosts or others, whether they are acting out of duty or loving-kindness; phrases like 'We felt we had to do something' sound like duty, but may instead express the strength of a compassionate feeling.

A person who, from any of these motives, regularly entertains others because they need it is a hospitable person – though the word 'hospitable' is too weak for especially saintly hosts. As before, if hosts are resentful we should sometimes call them dutiful rather than hospitable. But whether we should call them dutiful rather than hospitable depends on the reason for their resentment. They are not lacking in hospitableness if they are resentful because guests abuse their hospitality by wantonly damaging their property, but they are if they resent their guests' presence while feeling they have a duty to entertain them.

Hospitality to friends

Many people frequently entertain their friends (friends proper or intimates, rather than simply their circle). They do so because liking and affection are inherent in friendship (Telfer 1971: 224–7); the liking produces a wish for the friends' company (as distinct from company in general), the affection a desire to please them. But one can meet friends for walks and take them presents; why should liking and affection motivate hospitality in particular? The reason is that there is a special link between friendship and hospitality, one which I have already mentioned in connection with entertaining one's circle. Because it involves the host's home, hospitality (provided it is not too formal) is an invitation to intimacy, an offer of a share in the host's private life. When given to friends, who are already intimates, it has the effect of maintaining or reinforcing the intimacy.

However, there is a kind of paradox about entertaining the same people too often. If they reach a stage when they can 'drop in' and 'take pot luck', they scarcely count as guests and become 'almost part of the family'. Is turning friends into family the essence of this kind of hospitality, or does it go beyond hospitality? I think one might choose to say either. The important point is that there are two ways, each of which has its place, in which I may try to please my guests. I can either make a special fuss of them, or deliberately avoid a special fuss and make them feel at home.

As always, attributing hospitableness to a person describes them as going beyond the average. Friends are not thought of as hospitable merely because they often entertain each other, since this is to be expected. To count as hospitable in this sphere, hosts must be unusually ready to entertain their friends and unusually devoted to pleasing them. The same considerations as before apply about ulterior motives: if someone is always inviting his friends in to dinner simply to show off his cooking, he is not a hospitable person – but the friends may not mind, as long as the cooking is good.

Do we have a duty to entertain our friends? A hospitable friend will normally do this without acting out of a sense of duty. But it does not follow that we do not have such a duty; indeed, there are two reasons why we might assert that we do.

First, friends sometimes need hospitality. I do not mean that they are sometimes in need of it and with no other resources – people to whom one would be obliged to offer hospitality even if they were not one's friends. I mean that sometimes I ought to entertain people because they are my friends, though also in need of hospitality: for example, I may have a duty to entertain a friend who is lonely when I would not be obliged to do the same for a stranger in the same situation. We think of ourselves as having, even as having undertaken, special obligations towards our friends which we do not have towards strangers. We may also have a sense of a system of protection whereby everyone is looked after in this way by his or her friends.

The second reason for believing in a duty of hospitality to friends is based not only on the special obligations to friends mentioned in the previous paragraph, but also on the positive benefits of receiving hospitality, of which there are many besides the food and drink. I wrote earlier of the way in which sharing food with members of a group strengthens the bond uniting the group. In a similar way, if we share a meal with friends we include them in an informal ritual of fellowship, one which everyone understands. (Think of the kind of disappointment felt when a visitor who has not been seen for a long time cannot stay for a meal.) There are other psychological benefits too. When we entertain people, we do more than just provide them with company, which we might do equally well by visiting them. We also strengthen their self-esteem by our readiness to share our own lives with them, and we rest and refresh them by waiting on them and providing a pleasant atmosphere. (The quotation from Anna Thomas earlier in this chapter captures this aspect of hospitality very well.) In short, by our hospitality we can further our friends' psychological and physical wellbeing, and this is something that we have a duty to do. It is not such a pressing duty as meeting their needs. But it may be almost as important, because prevention of loneliness, self-hatred and depression is better than cure.

As I have already said, we can acknowledge that we have a duty to entertain our friends without necessarily thinking of duty when we do so. Sometimes, however, affection is not enough to motivate us. Perhaps we are too wrapped up in our own troubles to feel affectionate, or a friend's troubles are making him so unpleasant that it is difficult to feel warm towards him. But one can still make an effort, as we say, and entertain friends out of dutifulness. I argued earlier that such behaviour counts as hospitable although its motive is duty, provided the spirit in which it is carried out is generous.

But there is a special problem about entertaining friends out of a motive of duty. They are likely to assume that we want to see them for the pleasure of their company: are we being deceitful in entertaining them out of duty? And if so, how much does this matter? I do not have a complete answer to these questions. But part of the answer might be that this is a duty which we would not do for just anyone. So even if our actions do not have the spontaneity which normally goes with friendship proper, they are still the actions of a friend and we need not therefore feel hypocritical.

HOSPITABLENESS AS A MORAL VIRTUE

I now turn to the question of whether hospitableness is a moral virtue. In doing so, I shall make use of the account of moral virtues given by Philippa Foot in her paper 'Virtues and vices' (Foot 1978: 1–18). Foot claims that moral virtues possess three features. First, moral virtues are qualities which 'a human being needs to have, for his own sake and that of his fellows'. Second, they are qualities of will, rather than of intellect, situation or physique. Third, they are corrections of some common human tendency to either excess or deficiency of motivation. I shall consider the three types of hospitableness (hospitableness towards one's circle, Good-Samaritan hospitableness and hospitableness to friends) in the light of these criteria.

Foot suggests that whereas courage, temperance and wisdom benefit both their possessor and others, justice and charity chiefly benefit others, sometimes at their possessor's expense: 'Nobody can get on well if he lacks courage, and does not have some measure of temperance and wisdom, while communities where justice and charity are lacking are apt to be wretched places to live...' (Foot 1978: 2–3). Hospitableness resembles charity more than it resembles courage in that it benefits others rather than oneself. But would we say that a community without hospitableness is a wretched place to live, and that human beings therefore need to have this quality?

Perhaps hospitableness to one's circle and Good-Samaritan hospitableness are qualities which 'a human being needs to have'. But it would be more plausible to say that the corresponding fault is one which human beings need to avoid. If people are inhospitable to their circle, they do not entertain family, colleagues or new neighbours when they ought to do so. This is not a fault of great importance; society could rub along without the practice of hospitality to one's circle. But since it is a useful practice – one that promotes friendliness, and society works better if everyone does a certain amount of it – and since part of society expects it, one can call it a duty. If people are inhospitable in the Good-Samaritan sense, however, they fail to entertain those in need whom they have a clear duty to help: for example, motorists whose cars are stuck in a snowdrift outside the house, or victims of an accident in the street. Society is an unpleasant place if people are inhospitable in these ways, and indeed this is why such things are thought of as duties.

Inhospitableness to one's circle and Good-Samaritan inhospitableness, then, are faults which everyone must try to avoid. But that conclusion does not entail that we must all try to become hospitable in either of those ways. A hospitable person is one who entertains more than the average person. But not all such hospitality is a duty, and people are therefore not at fault if, instead of aiming at being positively hospitable, they choose other ways of benefiting those in need or those in their circle. Hospitableness to one's circle and hospitableness of the Good-Samaritan kind are as it were optional virtues, which embody particular moral ideals and are concerned with particular ways of making human life go well.

It might be said that the idea of optional virtues does not make sense, because calling a quality a moral virtue implies that everyone ought to cultivate it. I would defend the idea of optional virtues in terms of the old notion of imperfect duties, those which require us to choose between ways of carrying them out. For example, we all have a duty to help those in need, but in general we may and must choose which needy people to help and how to help them; so helping the needy is an imperfect duty. I therefore suggest that whereas we all ought to be compassionate, we have to choose whether to specialise, as it were, in Good-Samaritan hospitableness or in traits associated with other forms of compassion. Similarly, we all have a duty to be benevolent and to cultivate benevolence, but we must choose how to benefit our community: for example, whether to aim at hospitableness to our circle, or to aim at public-spiritedness. One cannot try to be every kind of good person.

The question of whether hospitableness to friends is a moral virtue raises issues that are more complex than those raised by the question of whether hospitableness to one's circle and hospitableness of the Good-Samaritan type are moral virtues. I distinguished two kinds of duty of hospitality to friends: the duty to meet their needs for hospitality and the duty to give them its positive benefits. Failure in the first duty clearly makes someone inhospitable. The second kind of duty, however, seems to leave some room for choice: perhaps we can give our friends some of the positive benefits of hospitality in other ways instead. In other words, the duty to help our friends might be regarded as an imperfect duty, and hospitality as one way among others of performing this duty. In that case hospitableness to friends, as distinct from merely avoiding inhospitableness to them, is an optional virtue: one branch of affectionateness. On the other hand, as I argued earlier, there is a natural connection between friendship and hospitality which makes it likely that a good friend will also be a hospitable one.

But are the needs met and benefits conferred by hospitableness to friends important enough to meet the first requirement for a moral virtue – namely that it is a quality which a human being needs to have for his own and his fellows' sake? One possible answer is that if the actions involved are duties, whether perfect or imperfect, a disposition to carry them out must be a moral virtue. But there is a problem here, because there is opposition to the idea of special duties to friends. It is sometimes argued that morality is based on universal principles, and so it cannot be obligatory for me to do something for some people because I am fond of them but not obligatory for me to do it for others. On the formal level, this objection can be met. My obligation is not based on a private rule that I must do things for particular people, but on a universal principle that everyone has special duties to his or her own friends. But there is still a question whether this principle is morally acceptable (just as there is with patriotism, which involves special duties to one's own country). How far is it morally acceptable to favour particular groups connected with oneself?

I sketched in Chapter 1 a general defence of the policy of favouring one's own group, broadly on the grounds that it is a universal human entitlement. Here, some points can be made in support of the notion that there are special duties to friends. First, friendship by its very nature involves taking on a special responsibility for one's friends. If this is so, anyone who thinks that there are no special duties to friends is arguing against friendship itself, and to abolish friendship would certainly make things worse for human beings in general. Second, there are some benefits which one can confer only on those to whom one is close – including, of course, the benefit of making them feel that they are valued for themselves and that one would not do the same for just anyone. Third, as I have already said, we can think of obligations to friends as constituting part of a network of protection and beneficence which raises the general level of welfare. If we can defend the existence of duties to friends in these ways, we can also defend the idea of a moral virtue of hospitableness to friends.

It might be objected at this point that, since anyone without friends is excluded from a network based on friendship, hospitableness to friends is not of general benefit. Admittedly it is not of universal benefit, but a society where people are hospitable to their friends is better on balance than one where they are not. However, what is of more general benefit than hospitableness to friends is a less exclusive kind of hospitableness, springing from friendliness as well as affection, and extended both to friends proper and to those in one's wider circle. Indeed, to a friendly person there is no sharp distinction between friends and wider circle. We might decide then that hospitableness which is confined to friends is a moral virtue; but that because of its narrowness it is a lesser virtue than the kind of hospitableness – probably what most people mean by the word – which embraces the wider circle as well as friends.

Foot's second criterion of a moral virtue is that it is a quality of will. Foot uses 'will' in a wide sense, to cover what is wished for as well as what is sought. The purpose of this criterion is to distinguish moral virtues from excellences of intellect and physique, and to imply that they can be acquired by anyone. My account of hospitableness, whether to those in one's circle, those in need, or friends, meets this requirement in that it depicts hospitableness as depending on devotion and a spirit of generosity rather than on skill.

We might wonder whether deficiencies of natural temperament could prevent some people from acquiring hospitableness. But in this respect hospitableness is no different from other moral virtues. In calling any quality a moral virtue we assume that over time most people could acquire the required disposition if they tried: that is part of what Foot means by saying that moral virtues are qualities of will. It may be true that some people are unable to become truly hospitable, but it may also be true that some people are unable to become truly generous or kind, as distinct from becoming able to mimic these qualities. Such people are not blameworthy, but we regard a quality as a moral virtue only if we think those who cannot acquire it are exceptional.

It might be claimed that circumstances, rather than temperament, could prevent someone from becoming hospitable. We acquire virtues by trying to practise them, but it might be argued that not everyone can practise hospitableness because not everyone has the resources with which to entertain. I have heard hospitableness called a middle-class virtue, presumably on these grounds. But it is not true that some people do not have the resources to entertain. Not everyone can provide lavish hospitality, or even conventional middle-class dinner parties. But even a beggar can be hospitable by sharing food with a newcomer. Admittedly homeless people cannot share their homes. But the most important part of hospitality is the sharing of one's own provisions, and the more needy a person is, the more generous and hospitable the sharing is.

The third feature of moral virtues, according to Foot, is that they help people to do what is difficult by correcting the excess or deficiency of motivation to which human beings in general are prone. All the kinds of hospitableness which we are considering pass this test, in that they counteract a common lack of motivation. Many of us do not entertain very much, not because we have chosen to pursue other virtues instead, but because we do not want to spend the time, thought or money required, or to have our privacy invaded. This is most obvious with Good-Samaritan hospitality, but even hospitality to friends does not always come easily. We might put the point by saying that hospitableness to one's circle, Good-Samaritan hospitableness and hospitableness to friends pass the third test because most people lack the motivation to entertain sufficiently frequently with the spirit of generosity which is inherent in these traits.

If some moral virtues, including hospitableness, correct deficiencies in motivation, it might seem that each such virtue is based on its possessor having a strong desire of a particular kind, which in many people is too weak. For example, compassionateness on this view would be based on a strong desire to relieve suffering. Such virtues would be distinguished from dutifulness by their characteristic motive, the strong desire in question: thus compassionate people help others because they want to relieve suffering, whereas dutiful people do so because they think it their duty. But if this is indeed the nature of those moral virtues which correct a deficiency in motivation, hospitableness as I have depicted it does not fit the pattern. I have not claimed that hospitable actions are all performed from one motive, nor have I claimed that their motive cannot be duty. All I have required is a spirit of generosity and the absence of an ulterior motive.

However, moral virtues do not obviously conform to this simple pattern. In theory we can distinguish between different motives, but a charitable, benevolent or friendly person often acts from a combination of motives, such as sense of duty and compassion, or compassion and personal affection. Admittedly, actions exemplifying a moral virtue other than dutifulness must be performed with pleasure, or at least with ease; as Foot says, the goal must be wished as well as sought. But the motive of these virtuous actions can still be a sense of duty, if by this is meant the sense of an obligation to help these people for their own sake, rather than an abstract respect for the moral law. If I help others out of duty and care enough about them to be glad for their sakes that I can help them, I am surely compassionate as well as dutiful. Indeed, it may be because I do care about them that I see their needs as imposing an obligation on me. Similarly, I have argued that if I entertain others from a sense of duty, but care enough about them to do so in what I called a spirit of generosity, I am hospitable as well as dutiful.

In this discussion I have set three kinds of hospitableness against Foot's criteria for moral virtues: hospitableness to one's circle, Good-Samaritan hospitableness, and hospitableness to one's friends. Are these all aspects of one virtue? On the contrary, they seem incompatible at first sight. For example, I cannot entertain my friends if my house is always full of alcoholics 'drying out', and I cannot offer my home as a refuge for alcoholics if I am always occupied with my friends. There is even a potential conflict between friends and one's wider circle, in that if one always sees friends in a wider context, this seems to involve a dilution of friendship (but we did observe earlier that the kind of hospitableness which includes both groups is better than the kind which was confined to friends).

Given these difficulties, moral agents have various options. They may decide not to cultivate any kind of hospitableness. All three kinds of hospitableness are optional virtues, so people are not at fault as long as they fulfil any perfect – that is, unavoidable – duties of hospitality. Or they may decide to aim at one kind of hospitableness and not the others, either because they are drawn that way or because of the difficulties of pursuing different forms of hospitableness at once. Again, they are not at fault provided they fulfil their perfect duties. Or they might strive to be all-round hospitable people, balancing the claims of different kinds of hospitality.

There are two factors which make this balancing easier. First, there can be claims of need among one's own circle of the kind that a Good Samaritan would acknowledge in any case. Second, the friends of hospitable Good Samaritans, if they are true friends, will sympathise with their Good Samaritan activities and perhaps help with them. A potentially alienating activity can thus become part of the friendship.

If hospitableness is an optional virtue, why would a person choose to seek this virtue rather than pursue other ways of doing good? One reason might be enjoyment: a person who enjoys entertaining has a disposition which will make the virtue easier to acquire. Another possible reason is talent. Hospitableness is not fundamentally a matter of talent, as we saw, but people may be moved to seek it by the thought that they possess talents or gifts of temperament that would enable them to be particularly useful in this way. An obvious talent in this connection is a talent for cooking; another is an imaginative taste in food, so that even when food is bought in for an occasion it is particularly interesting and enjoyable. A third reason is the possession of relevant gifts of fortune. Although lack of means does not prevent anyone from being hospitable, as we saw, the owner of a large or beautiful house, or of a fine orchard or vegetable garden, has something special to offer, and perhaps special obligations too.

But probably the most important reason why people choose to pursue the virtue of hospitableness is that they are attracted by an ideal of hospitality. This ideal is founded on a sense of the emotional importance of the home and of food, and of the special benefits which sharing them can bring. I have described some of these benefits in the course of the chapter. These ideas are common to all kinds of hospitableness, and show why there is a point in a separate concept of hospitableness, distinct from concepts of charity, neighbourliness and friendship. The ideal of hospitality, like all ideals, presents itself as joyful rather than onerous, and provides the inspiration for the pursuit of the virtue or virtues of hospitableness

DR JOHNSON'S VIEW

Can the merits of hospitableness be overrated? Here is Dr Johnson:

> 'There is no private house,' said he, 'in which people can enjoy themselves so well as at a capital tavern. Let there be ever so great plenty of good things, ever so much grandeur, ever so much elegance, ever so much desire that everybody should be easy, in the nature of things it cannot be: there must always be some degree of care and anxiety. The master of the house is anxious to entertain his guests – the guests are anxious to be agreeable to him; and no man, but a very impudent dog indeed, can as freely command what is in another man's house, as if it were his own. Whereas, at a tavern, there is a general freedom from anxiety. You are sure of a welcome; and the more noise you make, the more trouble you give, the more good things you call for, the welcomer you are. No, Sir, there is nothing which has yet been contrived by man, by which so much happiness is produced as by a good tavern or inn.'

> (Boswell 1934: 451)

Now it is easy to feel some sympathy for this view. But the mention of plenty, grandeur and elegance suggests that the host he is thinking of is trying chiefly to impress the guests rather than please them, like Mrs Elton in *Emma*. This kind of hospitality is not really hospitable.

Genuinely hospitable hosts, aiming to please their guests, will not cause them this kind of anxiety. (Though this is not to say that inept hosts who embarrass their guests do not exist.)

A more important point about hospitality which Johnson misses is the role of what I called Good-Samaritan hospitality. Going to the inn and calling for good things is enjoyable, but it does not do much to relieve loneliness and friendlessness, even when the bar staff take on their traditional role of confidants. In particular, an important benefit of hospitality, as we saw, is that it makes its recipient feel wanted as an individual. Being welcome as a good customer is not the same thing.

As for being able to call for what you please at an inn, one cannot help feeling that Dr Johnson has missed the point of hospitality. The pleasure of being entertained in someone's home is not simply that of having agreeable food and drink, which might indeed be better at the pub, but a complex pleasure which depends to a great extent on the fact that one is in someone's home. Enjoying this pleasure may call also on sensibilities that are not needed in the pub. But what is enjoyed can be at a higher level of experience altogether.

6   Temperance

SCOPE OF THIS TOPIC

In the previous chapter I discussed hospitableness as a moral virtue, one concerned with how we treat others in the context of food. In this chapter I shall discuss another moral virtue, temperance, concerned with people's attitudes towards their own food. The word 'temperance' is not quite right, but there is no unambiguous word for the quality which I wish to discuss. I am not going to talk about what is often meant by temperance, namely complete abstinence from alcohol. (This use of the word is an interesting case of what philosophers call 'persuasive definition' (Stevenson 1944: 206–26): the temperance reformers took over a vague but favourable word and gave it a new and definite meaning, thereby giving complete abstinence a ready-made verbal commendation). Nor am I talking about the broader Platonic virtue of *sophrosune*, the discipline of the passions by reason, often translated as 'temperance' in English. What I wish to discuss is the virtue which corresponds to the fault of gluttony: a virtue, that is to say, concerned specifically with food and drink. I shall not assume, as Aristotle did (Aristotle 1980: III, 10), that there is one moral virtue concerning food, drink and sex.

There are also problems with the word 'gluttony', which sounds rather formal and medieval. I shall use it nevertheless because it refers unambiguously to food, whereas the modern word for gluttony, namely 'greed', is also used much more broadly for being grasping about money or material goods.

I shall begin by considering gluttony rather than its corresponding virtue, because I think we are more inclined to recognise the existence of the fault than the existence of the virtue. It is possible to recognise the existence of a fault without believing in a corresponding virtue: for example, we may believe that there is such a thing as avarice without necessarily believing in a positive money virtue (as distinct from merely being free from avarice). My main aim in this chapter is to argue that there is indeed a moral virtue of temperance concerning food and drink, as well as a vice of gluttony, and that temperance is to be defined more broadly than is usually done.

PLEASURES AND SYMPTOMS OF GLUTTONY

Is a glutton simply a person who eats and drinks too much (leaving aside for the present the question of how 'too much' is to be measured)? It is true that one typical kind of glutton eats or drinks too much, not just on one occasion but quite often. But a tendency to eat or drink too much is not sufficient to make someone a glutton. We would not call someone a glutton if he ate too much because he always felt hungry; we would talk instead of disorders of appetite. Nor would we call someone a glutton if he ate too much for what we might call extraneous reasons: if, for example, he was under the thumb of a doting mother who was determined to fatten him up, or was trying to gain weight in order to play the part of a fat person in a film. The typical glutton is the person who says, 'I'm full up really, but these things are so delicious that I must just have one more'. In other words, it is the person who eats too much because of the pleasures of food and drink who is thought of as a glutton.

It might be objected that we cannot pick out a trait of gluttony, because the pleasures of food and drink are closely bound up with other pleasures, as we saw in Chapter 2. But this fact does not show that there is no such thing as a glutton. What it shows is that it may be difficult to tell in a particular case whether someone is a glutton or not. For example, if a person goes to far too many dinner parties when he should be spending more time on his work, it may not be easy to tell whether he is a glutton or simply overfond of company.

Is the glutton concerned only with the pleasures of ordinarily pleasant food, or can there also be gluttons for the more discerning pleasures of the connoisseur? In terms of excessive quantity the connoisseur is unlikely to be a glutton – eating too much tends to interfere with gourmet pleasures. For example, one can spoil the carefully designed balance of a meal by over-indulging in the pudding, and one ceases to taste keenly when rather full. Nor does one need to take more and more of a dish in order to appreciate it fully. There are special circumstances where a connoisseur might overdo the quantity: for example, if a buffet consisted of a great variety of exquisite dishes and he wished to experience them all. But this is an unusual case, and one binge does not make a glutton. However, there are non-quantitative ways in which gourmets can be gluttons, as we shall see.

In Chapter 2 I argued that the pleasures of food are predominantly the pleasures of taste enhanced by the pleasures of smell. What about a person who eats too much for psychological reasons: is he or she to be called a glutton? Here one needs to distinguish, no doubt roughly, between two kinds of case. On the one hand, there are the people who often eat too much because they like that cheerful feeling and improved morale, perhaps deriving from a rise in the blood sugar level, which goes with eating; I shall call it the cheerful food-feeling. This pleasure seems to be intrinsic to food, even if it is not what people first think of as one of its pleasures, and I think we would regard someone who ate too much in pursuit of it as a glutton. If, on the other hand, we think that food plays a partly symbolic role in a person's overeating and that the overeater is really 'hungry' for something else, such as affection or self-esteem, we do not think of him or her as a glutton.

Whether a person whose overeating is symbolic is guilty of some other moral failing is a separate question. Since we do not blame people for behaviour they cannot help, the answer depends partly on whether the behaviour can be controlled; whether it can be controlled may depend in its turn on how far the overeater understands it. But if such an overeater could control herself but did not (I shall return later to the question of what more precisely that might mean), would we think of the overeating as exemplifying a moral fault, or only as unsatisfactory behaviour? I suggest that we might not think of it as exemplifying a moral fault, and that this is because we can sympathise more readily with this person's motives than we can with the motive of the other kind of overeater – the one who pursues too assiduously the cheerful feeling that food gives.

Similar points arise in connection with alcoholic drink. If people drink too much because they like the taste of the drink, they can be regarded as gluttons. But an important part of our reason for drinking alcoholic drinks is, of course, that alcohol changes our mood: it has an enjoyable psychological effect. If we are pursuing this effect we may not be particularly interested in a drink's taste or smell. But, as with the psychological pleasures of food, we can distinguish two different desired effects. On the one hand, there is the ordinary desire to be 'merry'. On the other hand, there is the desire to drown one's sorrows, to escape from reality, and so on. The desire to be merry is morally speaking like the desire for the cheerful feeling that food promotes: we do not in fact call the excessive pursuit of it gluttony, but there seems no very good reason why we should not do so. But the desire to drown one's sorrows, to escape from reality, is a desire for something which is not to do with alcohol. As with food, we might blame someone's excessive behaviour if we thought he could control it, but even so we would tend to think that it did not show a moral failing – or at any rate not one to do with alcohol: in some cases we might think the person was being cowardly in failing to get to grips with some problem which could be solved.

In talking about whether eating and drinking behaviour can be controlled or not, I have avoided words like 'addiction' and 'compulsive behaviour'. This omission is deliberate. I have said that we do not blame people for behaviour which they cannot control, but I have not tried to lay down criteria for uncontrollable behaviour, addiction or compulsiveness, or to work out the relationship between these things. This is not because I think that there is no philosophical problem about these notions. On the contrary, I think that they are exceedingly problematic, both philosophically and in other ways. They are relevant not only to excessive eating and drinking, but also to deficiency disorders in eating, such as anorexia and bulimia. To deal adequately with these topics would require at least a separate chapter, and one which would take us beyond philosophy into sociology, psychology, physiology and feminist theory, as books like *Fat is a Feminist Issue* remind us (Orbach 1984). I shall therefore leave issues of compulsiveness and addiction on one side, and confine myself to what we think of as behaviour which can be morally assessed, whether it is pursuing psychological or physical satisfactions.

So far I have depicted gluttons as those who eat too much, though I have also said that this is not enough to define them. But gluttony does not always involve overall excessive quantity. There is a kind of person who tends to eat not too much overall, but too much of certain kinds of thing: for example, too many sweet, fatty or salty foods. If this is because the foods are particularly nice, and not because they are the cheapest or easiest to get, we have another kind of glutton. In fact a medieval tag about gluttony mentions no fewer than four dimensions of gluttony apart from excessive quantity. The glutton, it was said, showed his gluttony in eating 'praepropere, nimis, ardenter, laute, studiose' (too quickly, too much, too keenly, extravagantly, fussily) (Geach 1977: 133).

We can agree that all these kinds of behaviour are symptomatic of gluttony, provided it is from a desire for the pleasures of food that the person behaves in this way. The person who eats too quickly, not because he cannot wait to get to the delicious food but because he is in a hurry to get back to his work, is not a glutton but a workaholic; the person who spends too much money on food, not to get especially nice food, but to impress others with his wealth and sophistication, is not a glutton but vain, and so on. With that proviso, we can take the medieval tag as describing various possible types or manifestations of gluttony, and it is now clear how the gluttonous gourmet might fit in: for example, he might be too extravagant or too fussy. But all of these types of gluttony can be grouped together as cases of caring too much for the pleasures of eating and drinking.

BELIEFS AND DESIRES IN GLUTTONY

The phrase 'caring too much' is ambiguous. It might mean 'caring more than one should', with the implication that the glutton disapproves of his own conduct; or it might mean 'caring more than other people do', with the suggestion that the glutton judges differently from others, and thinks his behaviour is appropriate.

In his discussion of the broader vice of intemperance, Aristotle makes a similar distinction between weakness or *akrasia*, a failing but not a vice, and a vice properly so called. Weak people basically know that their behaviour is inappropriate; those with the vice think that their behaviour is perfectly appropriate (although others do not). James D. Wallace, in his book on the virtues, says that Aristotle's conception of the vice is incoherent, because it imputes to the intemperate person the incoherent belief that one should pursue every passing pleasure without restraint (Wallace 1978: 86–7). In Wallace's view this belief is incoherent because nothing, including pleasure, can be systematically pursued without some restraint. He concludes that intemperance must be what Aristotle would call a weakness rather than a vice: a trait according to which people behave excessively in their own view as well as that of others.

But the account of the intemperate person which Wallace attributes to Aristotle (not without some justification) is not the natural way to think of the glutton who considers his conduct to be appropriate. It does not follow from that description that such people think that agreeable food is the only thing that matters, or that agreeable food should be pursued unrestrainedly, regardless of whether that policy is coherent or not. All that follows is that they think that nice food, or if they are gourmets 'good' food, is more important than most people think it is. So there is no obvious incoherence in the idea of a glutton who considers that his conduct is appropriate.

Aristotle's distinction leaves us with two types of glutton: the one who cares for food more than he ought, and is therefore weak-willed, and the one who believes that his behaviour is appropriate, whom I shall call the principled glutton. But there is another possibility, and that is the glutton who believes in one part of himself that his behaviour is appropriate, and in another part that it is not – in other words, the self-deceiving glutton.

We can detect self-deceiving gluttons, like other kinds of self-deceiver, by seeing what they would say about someone else when their own wishes are not directly involved. They may find themselves condemning in someone else behaviour which they would condone in themselves, and thereby revealing that they do not at bottom think that their own behaviour is acceptable.

Let us return to the weak-willed glutton, the person who thinks that what he is doing is excessive and inappropriate, but still does it. The phenomenon of moral weakness, in the sense of thinking that one ought not to do a thing but still doing it, is one of the most discussed topics in philosophy. It seems particularly relevant to eating: Aristotle's discussion of it, which started the whole debate, is about eating sweet things when one thinks one ought not to (Aristotle 1980: VII, 3). I do not propose to discuss the topic at length, as many others have done so, for example William Charlton and those in Geoffrey Mortimore's collection (Charlton 1988, Mortimore 1971). I will say only that the phenomenon of weakness of will has seemed puzzling to some philosophers because of various assumptions which they make, such as that human beings are essentially unified and rational creatures. I think it is more reasonable to question these assumptions than to try, as some have done, to argue away so familiar an experience as weakness of will.

Wallace thinks that the weak-willed form of gluttony is one aspect of a broader failing, which he calls self-indulgence. He defines this trait as the tendency to be seduced by easy pleasures, and includes in it not only the weak-willed form of gluttony but also such examples as spending all one's time watching television instead of sometimes taking exercise.

This line of argument raises the whole question of the basis of dividing up virtues and vices. The self-indulgent person, as Wallace describes him, is one recognisable kind of faulty person. But not all weakness of will, or even all weak-willed pursuit of pleasure, falls under this description. Weakness of will, in the sense of doing what one thinks one ought not to do, can also be shown in strenuous and disciplined pursuit of pleasure. For example, suppose I conceive a desire for a particular elaborate and delicious pudding. I know I should be grading a pile of essays which I have promised to return the next day. Instead I spend the day hunting down out-of-the-way ingredients and concocting the pudding, which requires patience, careful timing and a steady hand. At the back of my mind I feel guilty, but I tell myself that now I have begun I would be wasting even more time if I stopped in the middle. This would be an example of gluttony which is weak-willed, in that I myself think that my behaviour is unjustified, but it is not self-indulgent in Wallace's sense.

In theory we can divide up our subject matter in several different ways. We can group together all actions, easy or strenuous, which are contrary to the agent's convictions, and call them weak-willed. Or we can group together all weak-willed indulgence (that is, indulgence contrary to conviction) in easy pleasures, including the pleasures of food, and call it self-indulgence. Or again we can group together all cases of the inappropriate pursuit of the pleasures of food, whether weak-willed, self-deceiving or genuinely principled, whether easy or strenuous, and call it gluttony. It is a question of psychological fact how far any of these traits has a real unity: that is, how far a person who is weak-willed in one area tends to be weak-willed in all, how far a person who is self-indulgent about food tends also to be self-indulgent about other easy pleasures, or how far a person who is self-indulgent about food when its pleasures come easily also pursues them with energy when they are demanding. For the purposes of this book, naturally, I shall group all the kinds of inappropriate pursuit of food together and call them gluttony. But I am aware that this may be partly an artificial construction.

MEASURES OF GLUTTONY

I now turn to the question of what counts as 'caring too much' about food. What is the measure of gluttony? One possibility would be to allow the glutton's own judgment to be the only criterion. On this view, people would be gluttons if and only if they themselves thought that their behaviour was inappropriate. This conception would entail that all gluttons are weak-willed people, people who do not approve of their own behaviour. Indeed, if this were the essence of gluttony we might feel that it was the weakness of will as much as the excess that was wrong with it.

But failing to conform to one's own standard of behaviour is neither necessary nor sufficient for gluttony. As I said earlier, if people are gluttons their judgments about their eating habits may be distorted by self-deception. I also said that there are people who have been brought up to believe in what to most people seems an exaggerated idea of the importance of food, and who have an enthusiasm to match. Their behaviour conforms to their own standard, but we still might think them gluttons.

There is also the possibility of standards which are bizarrely distorted in the opposite direction, perhaps under the influence of the kind of belittling of the pleasures of food which I discussed in Chapter 2. I am not thinking here of the special case of anorexia, but of more ordinary cases. I once knew a girl who had been brought up to believe that people were gluttons unless they always stopped eating at a stage where they could have eaten the same amount again. If she failed to obey this precept she would be failing to live up to her own principle, but no one would have thought her a glutton because the principle itself is absurd.

If the eater's own standards are not the measure of gluttony, how can we arrive at a measure at all? There are in fact three reasonably uncontroversial standards for what counts as gluttony. These are: damage to one's health or one's prospects of health; failure to respect one's obligations to others; and inability to carry out one's own plans. I hold that anyone who believes there is such a thing as gluttony has to accept these three standards: what can count as a standard if these do not? I shall discuss each of them in turn.

The first uncontroversial measure for deciding whether someone is gluttonous is in terms of damage to health: people are gluttonous if they habitually and knowingly eat too much or too much of the wrong foods (or too quickly) for the maintenance of their health. (It may be noted that excessive expenditure or excessive fuss do not in themselves impair health.) The health standard is important both from a moral point of view and from a self-interested point of view. As we saw in Chapter 4, if I have duties to myself or others (and everyone does), then I have a duty to keep healthy in order to be able to fulfil those duties; and if I have ideals of physical beauty or bodily harmony, I have a more direct duty to myself to look after my health. That constitutes the moral argument. From the self-interested point of view, if I have projects, it is in my own interest to keep healthy in order to be able to carry them out and enjoy them.

The standard of health must not be pitched too high. While it is plausible to say that a person who knowingly ruins his health by eating too much fat and sugar is a glutton, it is not plausible to say that everyone who knows his diet is less than optimally healthy (which probably includes most people) is a glutton. In other words, it is reasonable to trade in a small degree of one's prospects of health for an extra helping of the pleasures of food, unless a central project of one's life depends on maximising the chances of perfect health. Notice that I stipulate 'a small degree of health'. Where people's health or prospects of health are suffering a great deal from the pleasures of food which they have chosen to enjoy, their rational course must be to learn to like healthier food, and if they do not do this they are gluttons.

The status of health as an uncontroversial measure of gluttony, or rather for the avoidance of gluttony, might well be challenged. Surely it is sometimes intelligible to choose other things in preference to the preservation of one's health? People give the following type of example here: suppose a woman with breast cancer is told that her best chance of survival is to have a mastectomy and she refuses on the ground that she prefers to retain an unmutilated body even if this shortens her life. Surely this is an intelligible choice?

I agree that if there is an unavoidable choice between health and beauty, it is intelligible to choose beauty, and there are many other things which it would be intelligible to prefer to health, if the choice were stark and unavoidable. But the glutton's choice is not a stark one: it is the choice between ruining health for the sake of the pleasures of food and preserving it at the price of a modification of those pleasures. In such a situation it is surely irrational to choose to ruin one's health. For example, perhaps I think that a 'proper' meal has to have French-style sauces made with cream: I can have smaller helpings, or fewer proper meals, thus retaining both my prospects of health and my gourmet standards. Or perhaps I think that a proper evening out has to feature an enormous meal: I can resolve to have fewer evenings out, thus retaining both my health and my idea of a good time. This argument depends on people being able to modify their eating habits, but succeeding in this is not a rare occurrence.

The second uncontroversial measure is respect for our obligations to other people. This respect is partly shown in the care we take over our own health, but there are other aspects of our behaviour regarding food which affect other people directly. Our concern for the pleasures of food is excessive if it leads us to mistreat other people – and here fuss and extravagance may be as relevant as quantity. C. S. Lewis in his *Screwtape Letters* is very amusing on this point (Screwtape is a devil writing to advise his devil nephew Wormwood on the temptation of Wormwood's 'patient', the soul whose ultimate damnation he is trying to bring about):

> Your patient's mother, as I learn from the dossier and you might have learnt from Glubose [the mother's tempter], is a good example. She would be astonished – one day, I hope, *will* be – to learn that her whole life is enslaved to this kind of sensuality, which is quite concealed from her by the fact that the quantities concerned are small. But what do quantities matter, provided we can use a human belly and palate to produce querulousness, impatience, uncharitableness, and self-concern? Glubose has this old woman well in hand. She is a positive terror to hostesses and servants. She is always turning from what has been offered her to say with a demure little sigh and a smile 'Oh please, please. . . *all* I want is a cup of tea, weak but not too weak, and the teeniest weeniest bit of really crisp toast'. You see? Because what she wants is smaller and less costly than what has been set before her, she never recognises as gluttony her determination to get what she wants, however troublesome it may be to others.
>
> (Lewis 1955: 86)

But how far do our obligations to others extend? I am certainly behaving gluttonously if I promise to make someone a cake and then find it smells so nice that I eat it all myself. Similarly, I am behaving gluttonously if, instead of completing a promised task, I spend that time on getting nice food for myself – as in my earlier example of making a pudding instead of grading essays. But are we behaving gluttonously if we spend a lot of money on agreeable food for ourselves instead of eating more plainly and sending the money saved to charities? Whether such conduct is gluttonous depends on how far our duties towards others are to be taken to extend. I discussed this question in Chapter 1, and concluded there that while we have a right to happiness and self-development, we do not have a right to put unlimited indulgence in our own pleasures before any possibilities of charitable donations or activities.

At any rate, it may be said, it is uncontroversial that we care too much about food if we actually cause suffering for the sake of pleasures we ourselves get from food. I agree, but in fact people often do this. For example, a domineering husband may bully his wife into providing unnecessarily elaborate meals for him. And people happily acquiesce in cruel farming practices used to produce their food, rather than choose a diet which does not depend on cruelty but is less attractive to them.

Indeed, a common reason for failure to respect animal rights is not lack of belief in the animals' cause, but simply gluttony. I once said to a friend of mine, 'You know, I can't help thinking that there is something in the arguments in favour of vegetarianism'. 'Of course there is', she replied, 'but meat's nice'. Another friend told me that he had read Stephen Clark's pro-animals book *The Moral Status of Animals* (Clark 1977) in the train on the way to visit his parents, and as he read he said to himself, 'These arguments are unanswerable!' Then he looked out at the young lambs in the fields and wondered whether there would be lamb for lunch. So he concluded that Hume was right in saying that reason was the slave of the passions: in other words, that even if the arguments did point to the rightness of vegetarianism, they could have no force against his wishes. (Hume would of course have said that this was a misuse of his dictum, and pointed out that there is such a thing as the wish to be reasonable.) Both these people would be examples of gluttons, as measured by the second uncontroversial standard: their desire for nice food led them to do what they themselves admitted was wrong.

An obvious case where behaviour that is likely to cause suffering must be described as gluttonous is that of excessive drinking. In his book on the virtues, P. T. Geach writes as though too much alcohol does no harm unless one is about to drive, work machinery or do something requiring a lot of concentration (Geach 1977: 133–4). These may be the most obvious situations in which a person might wrong others through excess, but there are other important ones. For example, some people get quarrelsome and aggressive if they have a lot to drink; if they realise this, but continue to drink that amount, their behaviour is gluttonous (though as we saw earlier, there can be other reasons for drinking too much which would not count as gluttony).

The third uncontroversial measure of what counts as gluttony is interference with the ability to carry out one's plans. One way in which over-concern with the pleasures of food has this effect is through its interference with health, since good health is needed for most projects; we examined this aspect above. But there are other ways, not concerned with health, in which being too concerned with the pleasures of food can undermine people's capacity to carry out their plans. People who feel they must have meals at set times, or who need regular cups of good coffee, or who demand that the food available should be up to their own exacting standards, are limited in what they can undertake. So are those who drink or eat so much one day that the next day they cannot do what they had planned to do.

Of course, eating good food may be part of one's plan. But I am talking about the situation where desire for the pleasures of food has become a source of interference in one's plans, instead of being one factor in them. People who care so much for the pleasures of food that they are in this position are gluttons. I regard this measure as uncontroversial because it seems to be entailed by a rational approach to one's life: if satisfying a desire for a particular thing cannot be fitted into one's overall plans, that desire has become excessive.

THE MORAL VIRTUE OF MINIMAL TEMPERANCE

I now turn to the examination of temperance as a moral virtue. I shall use Philippa Foot's account of moral virtues, which I summarised in the previous chapter. According to this account, to be a moral virtue a trait must have three features: usefulness to its possessor and others, a basis in the will, and the capacity to correct a common deficiency or excess in human motivation.

What I called the uncontroversial measures for identifying gluttony already provide a basis for a virtue of minimal temperance: minimal temperance is simply the absence of gluttony as identified by the uncontroversial measures. I call this kind of temperance minimal because it prescribes nothing about the proper way to regard food and drink. If temperance is defined only in terms of avoiding gluttony as identified by the three uncontroversial measures, any attitude to food and drink is equally acceptable provided the uncontroversial measures are met. This conception of temperance is broad: on this view a person who fusses endlessly about his food can still be temperate.

Minimal temperance conforms to Foot's first feature because freedom from gluttony is useful both to the people who have it and to those around them. It encourages them to eat and drink healthily, to respect their obligations to others, and to maintain the ability to carry out their projects.

Foot's second feature of moral virtues is that they are qualities of the will, not of the intellect or physique. This implies that, in the long term, moral virtues are under our control: we can cultivate them, and we can be held responsible for having or lacking them. This is a problem for temperance. As I said earlier, perhaps the degree to which we yearn for the pleasures of food is not entirely under our control, even in the long term: it may depend on our physiology, or on psychological compulsions which influence us at a subconscious level. How far this is true is a physiological and psychological question, and therefore outside the scope of this book. However, what the philosopher can do is to explain that insofar as temperance is to be regarded as a moral virtue it must be thought of as a quality which is ultimately under our control. It may follow that not everyone can be temperate, and that the area in which temperance is possible for anyone is narrower than we are apt to think. But we believe that there is an area in which we do have control, so there can be a virtue of minimal temperance which conforms to Foot's second feature.

Part of Foot's second requirement is that the possession of moral virtues is a matter of what is wished as well as what is sought. This stipulation is her equivalent of the Aristotelian idea that the virtuous person takes pleasure in virtuous activity (Aristotle 1980: II, 3). If minimal temperance is to conform to this stipulation, then the minimally temperate person is not only one who eats and drinks within the limits that the uncontroversial measures require, but also one who is happy to do so. Those who manage it only with a struggle are not temperate but merely strong-minded. This requirement that the exercise of virtue must be wished as well as sought entails a change to my thesis that minimal temperance is simply freedom from gluttony. There will in fact be a difference between being free from gluttony, which is consistent with not behaving like a glutton but still feeling like one, and being temperate, which entails being happy in temperate behaviour.

What are we to say about the principled glutton, who believes that the pleasures of eating are exceedingly important, important enough to take precedence over obligations to others on occasions, and behaves accordingly? I claimed earlier that such people count as gluttons if their heart is in their gluttony, so to speak. But it might be maintained that, even if they do desire to be gluttonous, their gluttonous behaviour is based not on this desire but on a false belief, so by Foot's second criterion this is not a case of a moral vice.

Before commenting on this claim I must recall the distinction between the principled glutton and the self-deceiving glutton. There is no difficulty about saying that self-deceiving gluttons have a moral failing, because their false beliefs are the product of their faulty wishes, and so their gluttony is based on desire. But this does not apply to principled gluttons. I think that although it is natural to call such people gluttons, we cannot count their kind of gluttony as a moral failing, because it does not conform to Foot's second requirement of being a quality of the will. Because principled gluttony is based on faulty belief rather than faulty desire, it is not curable, or not at least by the gluttons' own efforts, in the way that moral failings are – since principled gluttons believe in their way of life, they can have no reason to try to change. Such gluttons are deluded rather than immoral. (They may of course be just as harmful to themselves and others as immoral gluttons.)

Foot's third feature of moral virtues is that they act as correctives to a common excess or deficiency of motivation. It is clear that minimal temperance corrects common excesses of motivation in the realm of food. But there are several motives in question: the ordinary appetite for food, the desire for pleasant food and the desire for good food in *The Good Food Guide* sense. All these are strong desires which can on occasion get out of hand, as we say, leading their owners to exceed one or more of the uncontroversial measures.

We might at first be inclined to think that ordinary healthy appetite, wanting to eat when one is hungry, never needs restraining. But this is too hasty. In situations of food shortage, for example, people who do not control a normal appetite will act unjustly towards others. However, this is one of those occasions where we cannot expect the exercise of a moral virtue to be accompanied by pleasure; the most we can expect is that it should reduce torment. Aristotle realised that enjoyment cannot accompany every exercise of courage (Aristotle 1980: III, 10). In a similar way, desperately hungry people who behave with honour and restraint at a time of famine are unlikely to enjoy behaving in this way, but if they are truly temperate they can meet even this situation with serenity.

I am not claiming that those who do not bear starvation with serenity are blameworthy. Temperance of this kind is an example of heroic or saintly virtue, to which few attain (Urmson 1958). Nor am I saying that a heroically temperate person will not be angry that he has been left to starve; it is hunger, not injustice, which heroic temperance enables him to bear with serenity.

NEGATIVE TEMPERANCE

So far, then, we have a rather minimal virtue of temperance, measured only by uncontroversial standards of food behaviour. But our conception of temperance would change if we accepted any of the arguments (outlined in Chapter 2) claiming that there is something wrong with the pleasures of food as such: for example, the doctrine in Plato's *Phaedo* that the only way to set the soul free from the body (as far as it can be so in this life) is to be emotionally detached from all bodily concerns, or John Stuart Mill's milder but still condemnatory classification of the pleasures of food as lower pleasures. These doctrines embody what may be called a negative attitude to the pleasures of food and would lead us to a much more uncompromising form of temperance, which we may call negative temperance.

According to these views of the pleasures of food, a person who is fussy about his food or spends a lot of money on it is gluttonous, even if he harms neither himself nor other people, because he is paying too much attention to what is at worst evil or at best of inferior value. This makes temperance an important virtue, as it is in Greek thought: a corrective, as Foot would say, to the powerful and pervasive attraction of pleasures which are inferior or illusory and which only distract us from what is important.

But it is difficult to argue that this negative kind of temperance meets Foot's first requirement for a moral virtue. Whereas it is obviously beneficial for human beings living together to have appetites and desires in the sphere of food which respect their own health and interests and the rights of others, it is scarcely beneficial for them to take as little interest in food as they can. This conception belongs not to a basic human good which everyone must acknowledge, but to one particular ideal of human life which sees the pleasures of food as a threat. I therefore reject negative temperance as a moral virtue, and turn to a more balanced conception of temperance which can be more confidently commended.

BALANCED TEMPERANCE

If we think about the role that the enjoyment of food can play in our lives, we may wonder whether there is a vice of caring too little about it, as well as one of caring too much. I am not thinking here of loss of appetite, which is a sign of illness or of misery of one kind or another. I am thinking of a range of attitudes which include rejection of this kind of pleasure and contempt for those who are interested in food or take trouble with it. If there is a vice of indifference to food, as well as one of gluttony, temperance would be a middle state, possessed by those who care appropriately – neither too much nor too little – about food.

This conception of moral virtues as means or middle states between two vices, rather than as simply opposed to one vice, is a well-known Aristotelian doctrine (Aristotle 1980: II, 6–9). It is often attacked, for example by Rosalind Hursthouse (Hursthouse 1981), and it is true that Aristotle does not succeed in making all moral virtues fit this pattern. But I think that in the case of temperance we can make good sense of it.

In Aristotle the pleasures of eating belong to the same sphere of virtue and vice as the pleasures of sex. As one would expect from his ambivalent and sometimes negative account of these pleasures, the vice of insufficient interest in them is barely mentioned, although he acknowledges its existence and describes those who do not care what they eat as not human (Aristotle 1980: III, 12). If we want to understand how there might be a vice of indifference to food as well as one of excessive interest in it, we shall get no help from him. Instead I shall combine some of the positive thoughts about food that I have been developing in this book with Foot's analysis of moral virtues, and try in that way to develop an account of a more balanced kind of temperance than those I have so far described.

As we have seen, Foot says that a moral virtue must be beneficial to human life. In fact, she tends to interpret this idea as meaning that the corresponding vice is harmful in human life. It is easy to see that gluttony as identified by what I called the uncontroversial measures is harmful, as I have shown. Perhaps we cannot claim that indifference to food is harmful. But at this point I would argue that a quality can be a virtue both because it prevents harm and because it promotes good. Minimal temperance was useful for preventing harm, as a corrective of the excesses of gluttony. A more balanced kind of temperance would not only do this but also be useful in promoting good, by way of correcting deficiency of motivation in this sphere. It would entail due appreciation of the pleasures of food, because this appreciation is beneficial to all, and because its absence, indifference to food, though not exactly harmful, is a lack. It will probably be clear why I wish to claim that a due appreciation of the pleasures of food is beneficial to all: it is a source of cheerfulness and interest in life for its possessor, a great aid to sociability and friendliness with all kinds of people and, in a host or a provider of food for a family, a help in making others happy. Indeed, the virtue of hospitableness probably requires that of balanced temperance.

The second quality of a moral virtue is that it is not a skill or talent, but a disposition of the will and heart. In this respect there is a kind of dichotomy within balanced temperance. No aspect of it belongs to skills or talents, but avoidance of gluttony seems more like a matter of the will, avoidance of indifference of the heart. This contrast is less sharp than it seems, however, because will does not mean 'will-power'. As I have already said, a disposition does not count as temperance if the self-restraint is grudging: those who have achieved virtue exercise it with ease, as we have seen.

The demands of balanced temperance are therefore rather difficult to meet. On the one hand it demands that we value the pleasures of food at their true worth, and this means partaking of them with enthusiasm. On the other hand it demands that we sit sufficiently lightly to them to be able to forgo them with serenity when a more important claim conflicts with them.

Foot's third criterion for a moral virtue is that it corrects a common tendency to a deficiency or excess of motivation. Minimal temperance corrects a common excess of motivation: gluttony, as defined in terms of the uncontroversial measures. The adherents of what we called negative temperance would claim that it too corrects a common excess, but we rejected temperance of that kind as a moral virtue, on the ground that its conception of excess is too extreme to make it a useful quality. Balanced temperance corrects both the tendency to excess, gluttony as defined by the uncontroversial measures, and the tendency to deficiency which we called indifference to food. The tendency to excess may be more common, but the tendency to deficiency is also found.

I should make clear at this point that there is no one motive from which all temperate actions are performed: as with the virtue of hospitableness, actions showing the virtue of temperance may have one of a number of motives. They are connected to each other by their relationship to the pleasures of food, not by identity of motive. For example, people can show temperance in deciding with equanimity not to have another cream cake because they want to preserve their health, or in giving up eating meat, with equanimity although they are fond of it, because they are concerned for animal welfare. People can also show temperance in practising with pleasure sensible habits of eating, even though such habits have become ingrained and are now not thought of in terms of temperance at all. If asked why they eat as they do, such people simply say, 'I was hungry, and that's what I felt like eating'.

People may also show balanced temperance in a more deliberate pursuit of the pleasures of food, whether from a love of agreeable food, in pursuit of an ideal of good food, or in pursuit of some wider ideal such as love of elegance or civilisation. The desire to be a temperate person is itself a possible motive for temperate action – though we would think it decidedly second-best as a motive if it replaced the proper one, as in the case of a husband who said he would not expect his wife to cook breakfast, lunch, tea and dinner any more because having so many cooked meals was intemperate.

But is 'temperance' an appropriate word for the quality I am describing? We tend to associate the word 'temperance' only with its harm-preventing aspect, and the thought that someone might lack temperance through failing to make his food interesting enough is an odd one. I toyed with expressions such as 'bonviveurship' and 'gourmetship'; it is no coincidence that one is tempted into Franglais at this point. But in the end it seems that 'balanced temperance' is the best one can do. For one thing, the French expressions do not capture the harm-preventing aspect of balanced temperance. For another, they suggest that the person who possesses balanced temperance must be dedicated to an interest in food. This would be a mistake: the reasons which make the good-promoting aspects of balanced temperance important do not demand any kind of specialised interest, but only a capacity for enjoyment.

Balanced temperance as I have described it is opposed both to a vice of deficiency – indifference to food – and a vice of excess – gluttony. So far I have defined gluttony only in terms of what I called the uncontroversial measures, and have rejected the claim of negative temperance: that we should take as little interest in food as possible. But even if we grant that that injunction is too stark, we might wonder nevertheless whether the uncontroversial measures are too permissive. In other words, we might wonder whether someone who conforms to the uncontroversial standards could perhaps still be too interested in food.

Asking that question is like asking whether an interest in sport, clothes or gardening can be excessive. Some people are passionately interested in such things, but provided that they conform to the uncontroversial standards, their interest is not excessive on moral grounds. It might of, course, be excessive on the grounds that these activities were not worth the attention paid to them or 'hadn't much to them'. But given how absorbing and long-lasting such pursuits can be, it is difficult to argue for this view: anything which fascinates people for long periods of their lives will necessarily have a certain richness about it. An interest in food has these qualities, and can therefore be an element in a worthwhile life.

Conclusion

In this book I have pointed out that for those of us who live in the First World, eating is usually not only a necessity but also a leisure activity, and I have claimed that we are justified in treating our food in this way. I have argued that we have real and extensive obligations to those who do not have enough to eat. But I have also claimed that we are entitled to aim at happiness and self-fulfilment, and that what we eat and how we regard food has an important part to play in the pursuit of both these aims.

There is a school of philosophical thought, stemming ultimately from Plato, which is hostile to any pleasures thought of as physical or animal, of which the pleasures of food and drink are obvious examples. I have endeavoured to rescue the pleasures of food from this hostility, and to re-establish them as genuine and valuable pleasures which have an important part to play in human happiness. I have also claimed that food is important for reasons other than nutrition on the one hand and pleasure on the other: what, where and with whom we eat can have many kinds of meaning, and in particular can enter into our pursuit of many different ideals. Similarly I have argued that cookery is not only a useful craft and an enjoyable hobby but also a possible art form and an element in the pursuit of many ideals, such as elegance, style, hospitableness and faithfulness to nature.

Morality has a bearing on food, as on everything else. I have claimed that as well as our duties to the starving, we have duties in the sphere of food to particular individuals and groups. We also have a duty to ourselves to choose and pursue ideals, some of which might include a particular approach to food. We have a duty, both to others and to ourselves, to maintain our health and therefore to eat healthily. And we have a duty to animals not to eat them. Qualities particularly concerned with food are hospitableness and temperance: hospitableness, I have argued, is a moral virtue but an optional one, while temperance is a non-optional moral virtue, one which makes wider demands on us than those usually associated with the word.

At the end of Chapter 6 I raised the question whether it was possible to meet the moral demands of temperance but still be too interested in food. I said there that the subject of food had a certain richness about it which made it a worthwhile subject of long-lasting and powerful interest. But I now wish to suggest that if food became the only or prevailing leisure interest that a person had, that person's life would be lacking important qualities. At a time when popular cookery writers and television performers (often the same people) command so much attention, this seems particularly worth saying.

I do not wish to unsay all that I said earlier about the significance of food in people's lives. As well as bringing great pleasure, the choices of eating well as a leisure activity and of cooking well as a hobby are exercises of autonomy in themselves, and the practice of them, with all the creativity and social elements that are involved, develop the personality or self. There is much more to either than to, say, beer-mat collecting or bingo – though no doubt there are those who would say that I have not understood the finer points of these activities. As well as all that they can offer in themselves, eating and cooking can form part of many ideals, as I have often said, and gain still more meaning in that way.

But there are three important things which these activities do not give us, or do not give us very readily, and which other activities provide more fully: these are solitude, timelessness and transcendence of self. I shall say a little about each of these values, and try to explain why they matter and why I think that in the end food falls short in respect of them. I shall begin with solitude.

By solitude I mean being alone. It might seem odd that I should now extol the virtues of solitude, having said earlier that hospitality was important precisely because it brought people together and dispelled loneliness. But there is a difference between loneliness and being alone, as has often been said. Loneliness, at its simplest, is not just being alone, but being alone when one wants company. Similarly, there is a difference between isolation and being alone. Isolated people are those who are cut off from others, either physically or because – although they are often with others – there is for whatever reason no ready communication between them and others. Isolated people are not necessarily lonely if they are contented with their isolation, and conversely lonely people are not necessarily isolated; they may have plenty of contact with others but not with those they would choose or at the time they would choose it.

I would maintain that loneliness and isolation are both undesirable things. Loneliness is quite straightforwardly a bad thing because it makes people miserable. Isolation is not so obviously a bad thing. It might be said that it does not matter if people are cut off from others unless they themselves mind it, in which case it is the loneliness, not the isolation, that is bad. But this is too hasty. We all need some relationship with other people if we are to lead normal human lives. Some people are more self-sufficient than others, and there is no prescribed degree of connection with other people; but anyone, however happy, who was entirely cut off from other people would be leading an impoverished life.

However, solitude, simply being alone, is not in itself a bad thing. On the contrary, I would argue that everyone needs solitude as well as company. We need solitude to enable us to think. We also need it so that we can be exactly what we choose to be. Although we need other people for our own development, as well as for themselves, being with others requires some adjustments and compromises, and also causes us to make other adjustments and compromises which are not required and may be undesirable. If we are to have a self, we need to have some time free of these outside pressures in which we can find out what we really think and feel and want, decide what we should do and assess which adjustments are worthwhile and which are not.

Now the problem with food, from the point of view of solitude, is that its activities tend to be social. Admittedly, it is possible to eat out by oneself, or to cook a special meal and eat it by oneself at home. But custom tends to be against this, and because of the weight of custom, eating alone tends not to bring the pleasure which eating in company would have – quite apart from the practical problem of getting served in a restaurant if one is by oneself and the place is busy, or of scaling down dishes designed for four or six people. A person whose chief leisure activity is food, whether eating it or making it for others, will find it hard to get enough solitude.

But there are other activities which either require or suit solitude. When looking at beautiful buildings or pictures, or the stars or a country landscape, or listening to music, we do not need company; and it is often easier to respond to what we are seeing if we are not also conscious of another person's appraisal (especially if it is their appraisal of our reactions as well as of the beautiful sights or sounds). With reading and study, we are even more on our own: no one can do them with us. I suggest then that these pursuits cater better for our need for solitude than activities related to food. It might be said that we can also find solitude without doing anything: we can sit quietly in a corner and brood. This is true, and we may need to do just this from time to time. But we may also need to dig into ourselves, as it were, by seeing how we respond to revealing and formative experiences when we are by ourselves. For this purpose contemplative activities are particularly appropriate.

The second quality lacking in activities connected with food is timelessness. This quality, or perhaps group of qualities, is difficult to define. What I have in mind is such things as a sense of freedom from restlessness or pressure of time, a sense of the suspension of time (what people call 'time standing still'), a sense of continuity rather than discreteness. These things are all valued. For example, when people say of an experience that time stood still, they are not merely describing it, but are pointing to a particularly precious aspect of it – and when they say of a relaxing holiday that they lost all sense of time they regard this as a mark of its success.

Now the activities concerned with food do not cater very well for our longing for timelessness. Our appetite for food is subject to a rhythm. We can eat our meals in a leisurely spirit, but we cannot go on savouring the mouthfuls indefinitely. The only aspect of food and drink which offers an element of the timeless is slowly drinking a fine wine – by itself, not as part of a meal. It can be savoured slowly, and unlike a mouthful of food it repays this treatment; there is no pressure to finish it before it gets cold, and there is no time structure governing the drinking, as there is in a meal. Cooking is even more timebound than eating. Many dishes have to be prepared fairly quickly – before the pastry turns oily, the green vegetables wilt or the air escapes from the beaten eggs – and cooked with one eye on the clock so that food does not spoil, even when there is no time constraint on the serving of the meal.

Contemplating works of art or nature serves us better in this respect. Looking at things is not an activity structured by time, as cookery is. Similarly, study (as opposed to writing a book or an essay) is an unstructured activity: we cannot do it for long stretches at a time, but if it is simply burying oneself in something which absorbs one, it has no timetable and can annihilate our sense of time. Painting or composing seem at first to be more timebound because they aim at producing a result: each activity is divided into stretches between the completion of each picture or musical work. But both can be carried on in a timeless way because they can be practised without regard for the result aimed at: for example, the amateur artist often paints a picture in order to spend a day painting, rather than the other way round. We can even discover a sense of timelessness while watching or listening to the performing arts, such as music and drama. Although a play is not a static thing which the audience can contemplate for as long as it wishes, a good play shakes us loose from our own timescale and imposes its own instead. Somewhat similarly, a good musical performance imposes its own world of time on us for the duration of the piece. This imposition of its own timescale, although it is not timeless in the way that contemplation of a picture can be, gives us a kind of holiday from the pressures of our own time-world.

Personal relationships can have something of this timeless quality too. Although they involve a series of encounters, a relationship does not consist only of these: it continues between the encounters, in the thoughts and feelings of the people involved. Intense relationships contain the experience of time standing still when the participants are together, and while the relationship continues there is often a sense that it will go on forever: not necessarily a belief that it will go on forever, but a suspension of the sense of the relationship as mortal. This quality does not, of course, belong to all personal relationships. In particular, activities concerning food do not acquire timelessness simply because they concern other people: giving a series of dinner parties is the antithesis of a timeless activity.

The third feature which the food activities lack is the capacity to enable people to transcend themselves. This feature, like the others, is difficult to define. Any absorbing activity, even beer-mat collecting, can make its practitioners 'lose themselves' in it. But what I am speaking of is the sense of being caught up in something which is not merely distinct from oneself but also very much more important: a sense of the sublime.

As we saw in our discussion of food as art, food does not have the capacity for sublimity; we are not in awe of it, or moved to tears by it. This does not mean that there is anything wrong with enjoying food; it only means that there will be limits to the form that this enjoyment can take. If we are seeking experiences which not merely take us out of ourselves, but also involve us in something which we experience as much greater than ourselves, we shall need to turn to spheres that I have already mentioned under the headings of solitude and timelessness: the major arts, study and the contemplation of nature. All these, at their best, have the capacity to make us feel that we are taking part in something much larger than ourselves. I say 'the major arts' because in my chapter on food as art I argued that food might sometimes be a work of art, but showed that any such art form remained a minor art. My reason for deciding this was precisely that food is not capable of arousing this kind of feeling of the sublime in us.

I have so far not mentioned personal relationships under the heading of self-transcendence. This is not because there are no self-transcending experiences of other people. On the contrary, for many people self-transcending experiences are pre-eminently found in personal relationships. But one might wonder all the same whether there is not something odd about a sense of sublimity concerning other human beings like oneself: must it not be some kind of illusion? I would say that there is an illusion (not necessarily a harmful one) if one believes that a fellow human being is objectively perfect. But if we have a sense that a fellow human being is in the end both utterly mysterious and infinitely valuable simply as a human being, we can understand the notion that personal relationships can contain a sense of the sublime.

Earlier in this book I rejected the Platonic account of the nature of human beings. But two of the three values that I have been discussing, timelessness and transcendence, belong to a Platonic outlook, although Plato would not have allowed the status of an ultimately valuable activity to anything except the pursuit of philosophy. It seems then that we need Plato after all: even if he is not right about what we are, he may be right about what we sometimes long for.

If this is indeed the case with timelessness and transcendence, and if we also need solitude, as I have argued, we need to allow activities which cater for solitude, timelessness and transcendence to have a place in our lives alongside more transient activities, such as those connected with food. This claim in no way undermines the importance of the place that I assigned to food in our lives, but seeks only to counterbalance the enormous stress that is nowadays laid on it and to point out some of its limitations. So two cheers for food!

Bibliography

Adams, Richard (1973) *Watership Down*, Harmondsworth: Puffin Books.
Aristotle (1980) *Nicomachean Ethics*, trans. W. D. Ross, rev. edn J. L. Ackrill and J. O. Urmson, Oxford: World's Classics, Oxford University Press.
Austen, Jane (1966) *Emma*, ed. Ronald Blythe, Harmondsworth: Penguin Books.
Beardsley, Monroe C. (1958) *Aesthetics*, New York: Harcourt, Brace and Co.
Benson, John (1978) 'Duty and the beast', *Philosophy* 53: 529–49.
Bentham, Jeremy (1962) 'Introduction to the principles of morals and legislation', in John Stuart Mill, *Utilitarianism*, ed. Mary Warnock, Glasgow: Fontana Press.
Bible, The (1611) Authorised version.
Blustein, Jeffrey (1991) *Care and Commitment*, New York: Oxford University Press.
Boswell, James (1934) *Life of Johnson*, ed. George Birkbeck Hill, rev. edn L. F. Powell, Vol. II, Oxford: Oxford University Press.
Brillat-Savarin, Jean-Anthelme (1970) *La Physiologie du Goût*, trans. Anne Drayton as *The Philosopher in the Kitchen*, Harmondsworth: Penguin Books.
Butler, Joseph (1970) *Fifteen Sermons*, ed. T. A. Roberts, London: SPCK.
Charlton, William (1988) *Weakness of Will*, Oxford: Basil Blackwell.
Clark, Stephen R. L. (1977) *The Moral Status of Animals*, Oxford: Oxford University Press.
Diamond, Cora (1978) 'Eating meat and eating people', *Philosophy* 53: 465–79.
Dower, Nigel (1991) 'World poverty', in Peter Singer (ed.) *A Companion to Ethics*, Oxford: Basil Blackwell.
Downie, R. S. (1964) *Government Action and Morality*, London: Macmillan & Co.
—— (1966) 'Mill on pleasure and self-development', *Philosophical Quarterly* 16, 1: 69–71.
Fawcett, Hilary and Strang, Jeanne (1971) *The Good Food Guide Dinner Party Book*, London: Consumers' Association and Hodder and Stoughton.
Foot, Philippa (1978) 'Virtues and vices', in Philippa Foot, *Virtues and Vices*, Oxford: Basil Blackwell.
Francis, Dick (1976) *High Stakes*, London: Pan Books.
Geach, P. T. (1977) *The Virtues*, Cambridge: Cambridge University Press.
Gilligan, Carol (1982) *In a Different Voice*, Cambridge, Mass.: Harvard University Press.
Gurney, Edmund (1880) *The Power of Sound*, London: Smith, Elder and Co.

Hardin, Garrett (1985) 'Living on a lifeboat', in James E. White (ed.) *Contemporary Moral Problems* (3rd edn), St. Paul, Minnesota: West Publishing Company.

Hare, R. M. (1963) *Freedom and Reason*, Oxford: Oxford University Press.

Homer (1946) *Odyssey*, trans. E. V. Rieu, Harmondsworth: Penguin Books.

Hursthouse, Rosalind (1981) 'A false doctrine of the mean', *Proceedings of the Aristotelian Society* LXXXI: 57–72.

Kant, Immanuel (1948) *The Groundwork of the Metaphysic of Morals*, trans. H. J. Paton as *The Moral Law*, London: Hutchinson & Co.

Kymlicka, Will (1990) *Contemporary Political Philosophy*, Oxford: Oxford University Press.

Lane, Maggie (1995) *Jane Austen and Food*, London and Rio Grande: The Hambledon Press.

Lappé, Frances Moore and Collins, Joseph (1988) *World Hunger: Twelve Myths*, London: Earthscan Publications.

Lewis, C. S. (1955) *The Screwtape Letters*, London and Glasgow: Fontana Books, Collins.

Midgley, Mary and Hughes, Judith (1983) *Women's Choices*, London: George Weidenfeld & Nicolson.

Mill, John Stuart (1962a) 'Utilitarianism', in John Stuart Mill, *Utilitarianism*, ed. Mary Warnock, Glasgow: Fontana Press.

——— (1962b) 'On liberty' in John Stuart Mill, *Utilitarianism* ed. Mary Warnock, Glasgow: Fontana Press.

Mortimore, G. W. (ed.) (1971) *Weakness of Will*, London and Basingstoke: Macmillan & Co.

Nozick, Robert (1974) *Anarchy, State, and Utopia*, Oxford: Basil Blackwell.

Nussbaum, Martha (1986) *The Fragility of Goodness*, Cambridge: Cambridge University Press.

O'Neill, Onora (1986) *Faces of Hunger*, London: Allen & Unwin.

Orbach, Susie (1984) *Fat is a Feminist Issue*, London: Arrow Books.

Plato (1955a) *Phaedo*, trans. R. S. Bluck, Indianapolis: Library of Liberal Arts, Bobbs-Merrill.

——— (1955b) *Republic*, trans. H. D. P. Lee, London: Penguin Books.

——— (1979) *Gorgias*, trans. Terence Irwin, Oxford: Oxford University Press.

Prall, D. W. (1958) 'The elements of aesthetic surface in general', in Eliseo Vivas and Murray Krieger (eds) *The Problems of Aesthetics*, New York and Toronto: Rinehart & Co.

Quinet, Marienne L. (1981) 'Food as art: the problem of function', *British Journal of Aesthetics* 21, 2: 159–71.

Rawls, John (1973) *A Theory of Justice*, Oxford: Oxford University Press.

Singer, Peter (1972) 'Famine, affluence, and morality', *Philosophy & Public Affairs* 1, 3: 229–43.

——— (1975) *Animal Liberation*, New York: The New York Review.

——— (1979) *Practical Ethics*, Cambridge: Cambridge University Press.

Stevenson, Charles L. (1944) *Ethics and Language*, New Haven and London: Yale University Press.

Telfer, Elizabeth (1971) 'Friendship', *Proceedings of the Aristotelian Society* LXXI: 223–41.

——— (1987) 'Leisure', in J. D. G. Evans (ed.) *Moral Philosophy and Contemporary Problems*, Cambridge: Cambridge University Press.

Thomas, Anna (1973) *The Vegetarian Epicure*, Harmondsworth: Penguin Books.
United Nations (1948) *Universal Declaration of Human Rights*, in D. D. Raphael
  (ed.) *Political Theory and the Rights of Man*, London: Macmillan & Co.
Urmson, J. O. (1958) 'Saints and heroes', in A. I. Melden (ed.) *Essays in Moral
  Philosophy*, Washington: University of Washington Press.
—— (1962) 'What makes a situation aesthetic?', in Joseph Margolis (ed.)
  Philosophy Looks at the Arts, New York: Charles Scribner's Sons.
Visser, Margaret (1989) *Much Depends on Dinner*, Harmondsworth: Penguin
  Books.
Wallace, James D. (1978) *Virtues and Vices*, Ithaca and London: Cornell
  University Press.
Whittick, Arnold (1984) 'Towards precise distinctions of art and craft', *British
  Journal of Aesthetics* 24, 1: 47–52.
Wilde, Oscar (1948) *The Picture of Dorian Gray*, in G. F. Maine (ed.) *The Works of
  Oscar Wilde*, London and Glasgow: Collins.
Wolf, Susan (1982) 'Moral saints', *Journal of Philosophy* 79: 419–39.

Index